MY LVOV

HOLOCAUST MEMOIR OF A TWELVE-YEAR-OLD GIRL

JANINA HESCHELES

CONTENTS

FOREWORD

The biological clock is ticking. My eyesight and hearing are not what they once were, and my memory is becoming blurry. The generation that survived the Second World War is reaching its natural end. Like for many elderly people, my thoughts go back to my hometown; to the people who have stayed close to me, with the feeling that they remain an integral part of a painful human history that won't be forgotten.

Today, "my" Lvov can be found in every place where life is destabilised, where people lose their families, where they are chased from their homes and villages. I recognise it in the boarded-up doors and windows of the empty houses in the narrow streets of *Wadi Salib* (Valley of the Cross) in Haifa. Their residents were pressured to desert them during the 1948 war.

My imagination recreates scenes from the past: terrified people running quickly down the narrow stone steps that lead to the port, shots being fired over their heads. Below, boats wait to take them to an unknown destination.

History has known several displacements of populations, but our tragic past does not give us the right to confiscate land, to destroy houses, or to uproot olive trees that have been cultivated for generations. It belittles the Holocaust to behave like this.

On the contrary, our future in the Near East depends on our ability to establish the conditions that will enable us to live together, without the cyclical return to violence and wars. That, today, there are demonstrators who shout: "Jews and Arabs refuse to be enemies!" gives me courage and instils me with hope.

Janina Hescheles Altman

Haifa, January 2020

INTRODUCTION

Another life saved from a bottomless sea of evil. This was not by chance, but thanks to meticulous underground work. This twelve-year-old girl was saved because she was part of the literary world. She was one of the people in the Janowski camp in Lvov who had been infected by the literary virus. In this terrible Nazi camp, this virus could have proved fatal at any given moment, but for Janina (or Janka for short) Hescheles it was the elixir of life.

Among the hundreds of prisoners in the Janowski camp, what would have become of this girl were it not for her yearning for poetry, for her desire to bear witness "in poems without rhymes" to everything happening around her?

The attention of Ilian (Michal) Borwicz (Ilian was the underground name of Michal Borwicz) was drawn to the poems that Janina used to recite in the evenings before the women in her group, by the light of the bodies being burnt in Piaski – the sand-dunes behind the camp, where they had been shot. In this way, contact was established between the young prisoner and the underground group operating in the camp. In Janka's diary, we frequently encounter the names Ilian, Wahrman, Grün, Jakubowicz, Fränkel, and Kleinman – all those who were bound together by their underground activity.

After he managed to escape the hell of the Janowski camp, Ilian Borwicz never stopped thinking of Janina. Thrown into the abyss of horror, Janina understood and sensed more than could be expected of someone her age. Getting her out of the camp became one of Ilian's priorities after his arrival in Cracow. He had his contacts in the camp, so the escape route was clear – Żegota (the Council for Aid to Jews) needed to do the rest. In August 1943 our liaison agent, Ziuta Ryshińska[1], went to Lvov to discuss the 'when' and 'how' with Wahrman. At last, in October 1943, Janina and Elżbieta were able to flee the camp.

Several weeks later, when Janina was in Cracow, we gave her a notebook and a pencil. This grey notebook, filled with large and clear childlike writing, was fortunately preserved after being carefully transferred from place to place, just like its author – but never together with her.

Like the author, it was guarded meticulously, as we knew that any piece of paper containing "suspicious" content could prove fatal. In the dozens of pages written by Janina Hescheles, everything was clear and simple, not suspicious.

It was impossible to demand of this young girl, who had escaped from the Janowski camp, to be careful about what she wrote – in doing so, we would have snuffed out that which was most essential: her childlike sincerity.

Upon reading the first pages, we understood the value of this diary. The author, who without doubt had talent and had mastered the art of writing, described her experiences not only with sincerity, but also faithfully recorded both names and dates.

For this reason, even though at that time saving a life meant risking the lives of many others, we did not hesitate to ask Janina to write down everything she had experienced in Lvov shortly after her escape from the camp.

Today we can appreciate the fact that she wrote while the realities of Janowski were still fresh in her mind, before a life of (some) freedom could blur the memories of the past years.

By chance, in the first apartment where she found refuge in Cracow, she did not need to put on a front, at least not before her hosts, nor to pretend to be someone else, which allowed her to write down her memories as faithfully as possible.

Of course, not everything was so simple. The young prisoner, a child torn out of the camp, exaggerated her degree of safety with undue optimism. She expressed this subconsciously during her first days in Cracow, which she describes at the end of her diary: "I couldn't believe that I was in a bedroom, lying in a bed, with nobody breaking the silence..."

After the Janowski camp, words like "bedroom", "bed", and "silence", which for us represented nothing more than routine, gave her an inflated sense of security. Hence the indifference and carelessness which, in the first apartment she stayed in (a room of ours which served only as a temporary refuge), meant she would leave little notes here and there, between the pages of some book she had been reading – notes on the camp, Piaski, Belżec, death, and yearning for her mother.

The diary was written and taken on its clandestine journey, although it was a somewhat different one from that of its author.

We fully appreciated the importance and historical value of this modest notebook.

For a year and a half – from October 1943 until the day of liberation – it was often hastily gathered together with other papers and transferred when the previous hiding place was no longer safe.

Janina also frequently needed to change her location and identity. After the first quiet months, she had to "move house" regularly. She became the daughter of a Polish officer and a Jewish mother – we had no choice!

Then, after the Warsaw Uprising, she became a refugee from Warsaw. She could finally decide for herself which identity she wanted, using her imagination. She spent the last months of the war in the pleasant atmosphere of the orphanage of Jadwiga Strzałecka[2], who had relocated the establishment from the ruins of Warsaw to Poronin, a village in the foothills of the Tatra Mountains.

We sent the memoirs to the printing press in their original form, without modifications – except for spelling corrections. In her compact handwriting, Janina described the lives and deaths of Jews under Nazi occupation, a subject so often discussed these days due to the huge library of documentation and testimonies.

Janina, writing in her corner, and hiding her notebook whenever the bell rang or when footsteps could be heard on the staircase, provided us with a document of great historic and rare psychological value.

The Jewish Historical Commission interviewed numerous children and some of the stories were deeply moving, but there was a crucial difference – the children who testified before the

Commission spoke freely. They were out of danger, in a free and safe world, while Janina wrote her memoirs while she was still immersed in the atmosphere of the camp.

During every meeting with us, she would ask for news "from there". In spite of her apparent assurance, she was no doubt aware of the danger she was in, all the more so since we hid nothing from her. We should therefore emphasise the maturity with which she spoke on certain subjects and the distance she kept regarding very personal and still painful questions.

In the new reality of life in the ghetto, as well as in the camp, the personality of this orphaned girl, who had lost her father and mother and who had witnessed the deaths of hundreds of people, was formed.

The "new order" was clearly characterised in her mind – the fall of some and the rise of those who replaced them.

For instance, Janina's uncle got the job of cleaning sewage tunnels through a bribe, and the barber who shaved the German commander of the town, could take over an apartment. But it was different for people who had no connections...

Her father's last words to her had ominous implications: "... be brave and never cry. Crying is humiliating, whether in joy·or misfortune ..."

Janina wrote: "When no one could see me, I cried without stopping." After the hell of the camp, she wrote about the group of women with whom she went to the showers outside the barbed wire: "As we passed through the town, passers-by and children would stare at us. Not wanting them to notice our sorry state, we would sing joyous marching songs."

Occasionally we saw trucks filled with young Jewish girls from the ghetto or camp singing cheerfully. Sometimes we would hear this type of comment: "... and they still sing, these Jews, what impudence!" Here is one of those "impudent" prisoners, a twelve-year-old girl, who earnestly explains why the condemned women were singing.

This rebelliousness did not come out of nowhere. This young girl, who would wander around the camp and listen to conversations in Ilian's cardboard-packing workshop, progressively absorbed the ideas of people who steadfastly resisted the savagery. In this atmosphere, the spirit of rebellion was born: Janina's resistance to her fate as a person condemned to hang. In her words: "Is this heroism? Must I be such a hero? No! I want to live!"

Hence her proposal in Cracow to be allowed to help the resistance movement, or her idea to buy a half-litre bottle of gasoline and hide it among the bedsheets when, after the Warsaw insurrection, there was much talk of the heroism of the children who charged tanks with bottles of gasoline.

We hope that these memoirs will not only be a historical document, not only another accusatory voice against the Nazi regime, but will also serve as material for teachers and psychologists. Let them consider what to impart on children who are mature for their age, deeply wounded, and very sensitive.

Written by Maria Hochberg-Mariańska[3], Zegota activist and editor of the first Polish edition of Hescheles' diary in 1946.[4]

CHRONICLE OF LVOV

13th century:

Lvov (Lviv in Ukrainian) was founded by Ruthenian (Ukrainian) princes as a commercial town at the crossroads of trade routes. It was settled by Ruthenians, Poles, Jews (whose origin was probably in the Khazar kingdom and Byzantium), Armenians and Germans.

After 1340:

Lvov becomes part of the kingdom of Poland.

1772-1919:

Poland is divided up between Russia, Prussia, and Austria. Lvov becomes part of the Austro-Hungarian Empire with the name Lemberg.

1914-1918:

First World War – Austria is on the losing side.

1919:

Battles between Poles, Ukrainians, and Russians for the Ukrainian territories. Lvov is occupied by the Poles. The Jews are neutral in this conflict, but the Poles suspect that they side with the Ukrainians and organise a pogrom against them. In order to explain the position of the Jews, the Jewish-Zionist newspaper, *Chwila*, is founded. Henryk Hescheles, Janina's father, becomes a member of the editorial board, and chief editor in the 1930s.

1919-1939:

In Lvov about half the population are Poles, a third are Jewish (110,000) and about 20 percent are Ukrainians. In the surrounding countryside, the majority are Ukrainians.

23 August 1939:

The Molotov-Ribbentrop accord to partition Poland between Germany and the Soviet Union is signed.

1 September 1939:

The German army invades Poland. The outbreak of the Second World War. Henryk Hescheles flees from Poland.

17 September 1939:

The Soviet army enters Lvov. Henryk decides to return to his family in Lvov and is arrested by Soviet border police. After a year and a half, he is released from prison.

22 June 1941:

Operation Barbarossa. Germany invades the Soviet Union. On

their retreat, the Soviet forces set fire to all prisons in Lvov. Most of the prisoners perish.

30 June 1941:

German forces, including the Ukrainian Brigade *Nachtigal* (Nightingale), whose soldiers wear Wehrmacht uniforms, and a German *Einsatz Kommando* (Special Operations Force), enter Lvov.

30 June-3 July 1941:

First pogrom in Lvov during which 4,000 Jews are killed, among them Janina's father. Polish intellectuals are also murdered, according to a list prepared in advance.

8 June 1941:

A decree is published obliging Jews from the age of fourteen to wear a white arm-band inscribed with a blue Magen David ("Star of David").

22 June 1941:

A decree is published on the establishment of a *Judenrat*. Józef Parnas is its first head, Adolf Rotfeld his deputy. The *Judenrat* is ordered to pay a ransom of 20 million rubles within two weeks.

25-27 July 1941:

Petliura pogrom during which 2,000 Jews are murdered, among them Janina's uncle. Most of the synagogues are set on fire.

September 1941:

Industrial military plants (*Deutsche Ausrüstungswerke* or D.A.W.) are built on Janowska Street.

2 October 1941:

The Janowski concentration camp is set up. Dr. Parnas, the first head of the *Judenrat*, is executed following his refusal to supply young men to the Germans for the concentration camp. His deputy, Adolf Rotfeld, is appointed head of the *Judenrat*.

8 November 1941:

Most of the Jewish population is concentrated between the streets of Zamarstynowska and Szpitalna. In the underpass, beneath the Pełtavna bridge – called the Bridge of Death – 5,000 Jews are killed.

20 January 1942:

The Wannsee Conference. The Nazi leadership meets in Wannsee, a suburb of Berlin, and adopts a resolution calling for "The Final Solution of the Jewish Question" through the extermination of the Jews.

February 1942:

Adolf Rotfeld dies of a heart attack. His successor, Henryk Landesberg, becomes head of the *Judenrat*.

March-April 1942:

In the course of an "Action against asocial elements" (according to lists of people who received communal aid) 15,000 are sent to the Bełżec extermination camp. The Rabbinical Council had opposed handing over lists of the needy.

24 June 1942:

In the course of a swift twelve-hour *Aktion*, 6,000-8,000 people are deported.

10-31 August 1942:

The "Great *Aktion*" (known also as the August *Aktion*). 50,000 people from Lvov and its surroundings are sent to the Belżec extermination camp. Most of Janina's family are killed.

1 September 1942:

Henryk Landesberg, head of the *Judenrat*, and eleven Jewish policemen are hanged from balconies of the Jewish community centre.

January 1943:

The ghetto becomes a *Julag* or Jewish workcamp. Communal institutions are closed down and their workers murdered.

2-16 June 1943:

Liquidation of the ghetto in Lvov. Death of Janina's mother. Janina slips into the Janowski camp, into the last surviving group of Jews in Lvov and Galicia.

13 October 1943:

On the request of Michał Borwicz, the underground Council for Aid to Jews, Żegota, helps Janina to escape from the camp. Members of Żegota give Janina a notebook and pencil and ask her to write down all that she remembers. These notes form the main part of this book.

19 November 1943:

Liquidation of the Janowski camp. Lvov is declared to be "free of Jews" (*Judenrein*).

March 1944 until the end of the war:

Janina is in the orphanage of Jadwiga Strzałecka in Poronin, in the Tatra foothills in the south of Poland.

24 July 1944:

The Soviet army recaptures Lvov. The Polish inhabitants are transferred to Poland, mainly to the lands in the west from which the Germans have been expelled. An estimated 100,000 to 150,000 Poles were removed from Lvov. The town is repopulated by Ukrainians and Russians (including many Jews from Russia), who were attracted to it because of the many apartments that had been vacated.

1946:

The Jewish Historical Commission in Cracow publishes Janina's diary *Through the eyes of a twelve-year-old girl*.

February 1946:

The town of Lvov is incorporated into the Ukrainian Republic of the Soviet Union in accord with the Yalta Agreements. It receives its official Ukrainian name: Lviv.

PHOTOS

Janina as a child

Janina and her mother (1935)

Janina and her father (1936)

Janina and her parents (1941)

Fig 1. Lvov Center 1941-1943

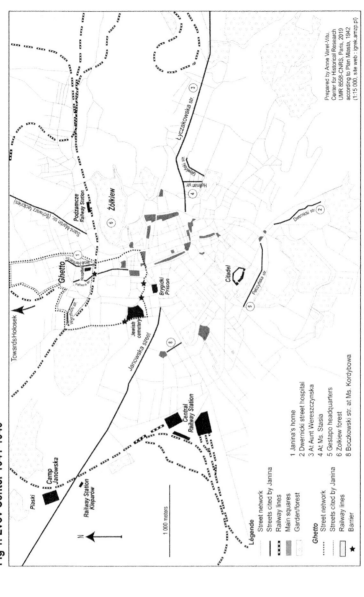

Légende

Street network
Streets cited by Janina
Railway lines
Main squares
Garden/forest

Ghetto
Street network
Streets cited by Janina
Railway lines
Barrier

1 Janina's home
2 Dwernicki street hospital
3 At Aunt Wereszczynska
4 At Ms. Stasia
5 Gestapo headquarters
6 Zόłkiew forest
8 Boczkowski str. at Ms. Kordybowa

Prepared by Anne Varet-Vitu,
Center for Historical Research
UMR 8558-CNRS, Paris, 2019
according to Plan Miasta, 1942
(1:15 000, site web : igrek.amzp.pl)

Fig 2. Lvov Centre, 1941-1943

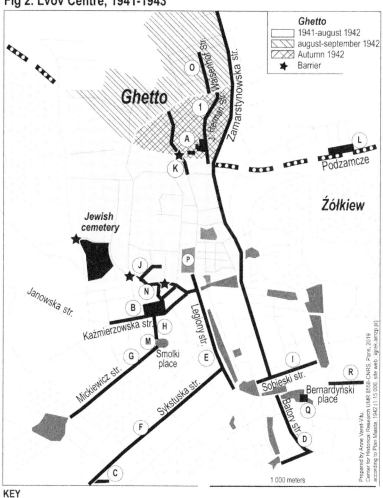

Legend:

Ghetto
- 1941-august 1942
- august-september 1942
- Autumn 1942
- ★ Barrier

Ghetto

Żółkiew

Podzamcze

Jewish cemetery

Janowska str.

Kaźmierzowska str.

Mickiewicz str.

Smolki place

Sykstuska str.

Legiony str.

Sobieski str.

Bernardyński place

Batory str.

Prepared by Anne Varet-Vitu,
Center for Historical Research UMR 8558-CNRS, Paris, 2019
according to Plan Miasta, 1942 (1:15 000, site web : igrek.amzp.pl)

1 000 meters

KEY

| Street network |
| Streets cited by Janina |
| Railway lines |
| Main squares |
| Garden/forest |

A Jewish Hospital Kusiewitcz str.
B Brygidki prison
C Prison at Lacki str.
D Ouprav-dom
E-H Streets walked through during the June 1941 Pogrom
H Kollataj str.

I Sobieski School
J Hospital, Alembeks str.
K Death bridge (Todbrucke)
L Podzamsze station
M Smolki square : the Schutzpolizei (police) station

N Szpitalne str. (showers)
O Prison at Waisenhof str
P Solski square known as Smugglers' square
Q Bemardynski square
R Lyczkowska str. At Mrs. Piotrowska

1 FATHER COMES HOME

It was the most wonderful moment. Somebody was trying to wake me up with kisses. I brushed them away and muttered, "I want to sleep, Grandpa." But the man persisted. I was surprised as I wasn't used to getting so much affection and it wasn't like Grandpa to kiss me. I rubbed my eyes and when I saw that the bald man before me was not Grandpa, I started getting annoyed. After all, Father only appeared in dreams and he was far away, in Siberia.

The bald man continued hugging and kissing me. I noticed that he was old and dirty, and dressed in rags. Steadying my gaze on his face, I was able to make out the dear features that I had so often missed, and began to cry.

Meanwhile, Mother stood by the bed, pale and speechless, watching us. All three looked around in disbelief. Tatusch (Father's nickname) couldn't believe he was here, with his wife and his daughter, in a furnished bedroom with a shiny floor.

The first night we were reunited was spent in silence.

Only much later did I understand what had happened. In September 1939, my father and his brother, Mundek, who was also a journalist at *Chwila*, had fled Lvov in the face of the advancing Germans, and had now returned home.

Since we'd been thrown out of our flat in Lvov and had moved in with Grandpa and Grandma in the Jewish Quarter at 14 Jakub-Herman Street, opposite the windmill,

I had to get up at 5 o'clock in the morning; the Polish school that I went to was far away. By the time I'd finished braiding my hair, it would be half past five and there would be no time left for breakfast. Mother, Father and I would tiptoe through the room where Grandpa and Grandma were sleeping so that we wouldn't wake them up. We would leave together, Mother to the hospital where she worked, and me to school. Father, who was back home now, would accompany us as far as the tramway and kiss us goodbye before we parted ways.

Mother's work and my school started at 7 o'clock. At midday, I always went to the hospital to see her, to have lunch and do my homework. While she worked at the hospital, I stayed with Aunt Reiss, Father's cousin, on Fredry Street. Her friend Jadzia Piotrowska would take me there after school. Afterwards, I attended ballet classes at the theatre, and then returned home by 6 o'clock.

At home, I would find Father lying on the couch in the smoke-filled living room. I would turn out the light and lie down comfortably beside him. Mother would not get home before 10 o'clock because after work she attended a class on the history of the communist party. The three of us would have a late dinner together and then lie in bed – with me in the middle for some time. This was the best part of the day for me. After a while, I would move over to the couch where Father would sing me to sleep.

Life in prison had really weakened his nervous system and he couldn't sleep at night. He would go from Mother's bed to my couch and smoke continually. He couldn't find work. He went to Trouskavets, a village nearby, but came back unsuccessful two days later, having found no work.

On Sundays, Mother thoroughly cleaned the room while Father and I went out. We would either go to have an ice cream at Zalewski's or just walk around town.

The people who knew us were too scared to say hello because Father had been in prison. They simply pretended they hadn't seen us. Even Father's cousin, who had solemnly promised to take care of us while he was away, chose to ignore us the first time she saw us in the street.

Father had three friends: Rotfeld, Jolles, and Bristiger. Before the war, Dr. Kurzrok, a business relation, used to send Father all sorts of articles to be published in the paper. My father was chief editor of *Chwila* (*The Moment*)[1], a daily Jewish newspaper that was published before the war in Polish. Dr. Kurzrok was filling in as dean of the medical school and Father was planning on asking him for help with finding work. But then, suddenly, war broke out.

2 THE GERMANS ENTER THE CITY: THE FIRST POGROM

On 22 June 1941 the Germans attacked the Soviet army ('Operation Barbarossa'), and the Russians began to retreat from the city as the Germans were approaching.

Mother took Father to his brother's wife, Aunt Marysia, at Lyczakowska Street, so that he could stay there until the situation in town had calmed down. Aunt Marysia, however, wasn't home. She and her daughters had found shelter from the explosions in Glowinski Street, so Father stayed there alone.

The Germans arrived on a Monday, 30 June 1941.

Mamoushia, as we called Mother, used to work as a secretary at the hospital on 54 Dwernicki Street, but since the outbreak of the war she was employed as a nurse.

She went to the hospital but was worried about leaving Grandpa and Grandma alone.

Mother was relieved that she did not need to worry about

Father. I was still at home since Mrs. Jadzia Piotrowska hadn't come to fetch me.

Throughout the day, and well into the night, we heard explosions.

On Tuesday, at 4.30 in the morning, somebody knocked on the door while we were still asleep. I thought perhaps this would be Mrs. Jadzia, but it was Father who brought us some lard and bread rolls from my aunt's house. He asked us to get dressed and we stepped out.

What we saw was an entirely different city, a Lvov after the explosions. The city was unrecognisable. Ukrainian blue and yellow flags fluttered above the front gates. Shopfront shutters were destroyed and Jewish shops had been looted. The streets were filled with cars and bicycles were decked out with flowers.

We crossed the city afoot to go and see one of Father's friends, Adolph Rotfeld, on Batory Street. Mr. Rotfeld was responsible for managing the buildings in the neighbourhood. He had been given orders to turn in all radios.

Father advised him to burn all the registers so it would be harder for the Germans to know who owned a radio. Father and Mr. Rotfeld started arguing, and in the end Mr. Rotfeld decided to go and turn in his radio. Father refused to do so and set off to a meeting at Rabbi Levin's house about setting up a *Judenrat* (Jewish community council). Mr. Rotfeld had warned Father against going to the meeting.

I was walking next to Father while Mr. Rotfeld was carrying his radio alongside his clerk. The streets were full of Ukrainians armed with wooden and iron clubs and we could hear shouting from far away.

On the corner of Legony Street, Father bumped into a friend and stopped to talk to her. Mr. Rotfeld kept walking. After a few minutes, the clerk who had been helping Mr. Rotfeld came back and muttered a few words in German. Father changed direction and we continued via Sykstuska Street. He was looking worried so I asked him what had happened, but he wouldn't say.

In front of the post office, there were people with spades and the Ukrainians were hitting Jews and shouting, "*Jude! Jude!*"

Father changed direction again and headed to Mickiewicz Street to visit another friend, Dr. Jolles. They sat me down in an armchair and gave me books and sweets while they talked quietly in a corner.

All the whispering surprised me. Outside the window, we could hear shouting. Father jumped up from his seat, looked at his watch, and left with me.

We were stopped by Mrs. Nunia Blaustein, who was standing in the entrance to the building. She begged us not to leave, saying it was dangerous for us to be outside. She herself had been stopped by the Ukrainians and had been harassed. They had only let her go when she told them she was on her way back from church.

Father kissed me and said, "Yania, you are ten years old now and it's up to you to be independent. Don't pay attention to what other people are doing. It's up to you to be brave." He kissed me again and said he had to leave.

It began to sink in. I wanted to cry but he said, "If you love me, off you go, be brave and *never* cry. Crying is humiliating, whether from happiness or sadness. Go home now and leave me here."

I hugged and kissed him for the last time and left. When I got to the corner of the street, I glanced back. I saw Father standing by the front gate, blowing kisses to me from afar.

I crossed Kolontai Street, which is where Father was supposed to get to for the meeting with Rabbi Levin. The street was full of young men who were beating up Jews with bats, brooms, and stones. They took the Jews over to Kazimierowska Street in Brygidki.

I ran through that part of the street and turned into Legionov. Here, too, the avenue was full of Jews getting beaten up. Here, too, people were being taken away to Brygidki to clear up the corpses.

I wanted to go back to Zamarstynowska, but I continued on to Pshedshkola Street. I saw six-year-old children pulling hair from women's heads and men's beards. The shouting and crying got louder and louder.

I shut my eyes, covered my ears, and ran for home as fast as I possibly could.

Finally, I arrived. Everyone in our building was worried. No one dared to go outside.

Suddenly, some Ukrainians burst into the building and started throwing people out, saying they were taking them to work.

Grandma was ill. Grandpa and a neighbour came into our room while Grandma blocked the front door with a cupboard. Bibrowa, our neighbour, hid with us too and left her children with neighbours. No women or children were touched, but all the men were taken from the building. They returned in the evening, covered in blood. They had been forced to hand over all the valuables they had had on them.

It was 6 o'clock. Mrs. Piotrowska still hadn't arrived and Father hadn't come back either. I thought he'd gone to see Aunt Marysia. The shouting in the streets hadn't stopped.

Grandma suggested I go to bed but I didn't get undressed. The whole night I sat on the couch in my dress.

The next morning, on the Wednesday, someone knocked on the door. Because I thought it was Father, I was happy, but it turned out to be our neighbour, Wurzl, who had come to warn us that people were getting arrested again on Zamarstynowska Street.

An hour later, someone else knocked on the door. It was Mrs. Piotrowska, who had finally come. She fetched me at Grandma's house and brought me to Aunt Marysia, who, in the meantime, had returned home together with her daughters. Both girls were blonde, one was ten and the other was nine years old.

Mamoushia arrived in the afternoon. When she found out Father wasn't there, she decided to go to Mr. Rotfeld's. She found that he'd been brutally blinded and had broken ribs, but she couldn't get any information from him. She then went to the Rabbi Levin family's house but only Mrs. Levin was there. Mrs. Levin said her husband had gone to Szeptycki and hadn't come back – Szeptycki was a Patriarch of the Greek-Catholic Church.

We could not locate Father, so we were getting worried. When Mr. Rotfeld had recovered somewhat from his injuries, he told Mother that he had been beaten up at the prison on Lontski Street but hadn't seen Father there. Some people we knew who had been taken that Monday to the prison on Pelczynska Street told Mother that Father wasn't there either, nor was he in the other prison on Zamarstynowska Street.

Mother found out that 200 people had been shot in

8

Kazimierzowska Street in Brygidki. Some people said that they had seen Father together with Rabbi Levin, coming back from Szeptycki's. Others said that they had seen Levin's body thrown down at the entrance to his house. Others again, claimed to have seen Levin's body at Brygidki, but nothing was really certain.

After a week, I returned back home to Grandma's house.

Jews were ordered to pay 200,000 rubles in two payments within two weeks. The *Judenrat* was set up. The president was Joseph Parnes, his deputy was Adolph Rotfeld, and there were seven *Judenrat* members. Everyone over fourteen was ordered to wear an armband.

Mother was fired from the hospital because she was Jewish. Now, she had to be careful not to get caught. When the streets were quiet, we went to the house of her brother, Jerzy Blumenthal. Aunt Sala Blumenthal always prepared potatoes and vegetables because they were easier to find in her neighbourhood.

Sometimes I went to the Blumenthal's with my cousin, Klara, who was sixteen. Klara would take her armband off as we approached the fish store to join the queue. She came to see us every week with her twelve-year-old brother Gustak and her father. Her mother had died before the war, which had been a serious blow to Gustak, who loved his mother dearly. When she died, he developed a nervous illness.

One morning, Thursday, July 26th, Mother decided to go to Uncle Jerzy's. The streets seemed quiet. We stepped out of the house. At the gate, a man without shoes lay on the ground, moaning and covered in blood. Suddenly, two young men wearing blue and yellow armbands came towards us and shouted, "Get to work, lady! The kid goes back home!"

I went back into the house and Mother went to the Sobieski School to clean floors. Fortunately, she had found work again, but I was worried about her. She came back home tired and hungry but there was nothing to eat.

The next day wasn't calm either. People were getting caught all over the place. There was a pogrom going on because the Ukrainian Symon Petliura had been killed by a Jew in Paris. (His assassination took place back in 1926.)

That evening, there was a knock on the door. Our neighbour was standing on the doormat with Gustak in his arms – he was unconscious and his face looked swollen and grey. We lay him down, undressed him and took care of him until he came around. His shoulder was bleeding and his whole body was purple from the blows he had received.

On his way home from the *Judenrat* building, where he worked as a courier, he had been caught by a group of Ukrainians and taken over to the Lontski prison together with some others. There he got beaten up for no apparent reason until he managed to escape.

People even got caught on Saturday. Sunday was calm.

I went to find out about Klara and Uncle Mundek. Fortunately, it appeared that they were safe and sound.

When I went to see Aunt Sala, I found her crying. On Friday, during the pogrom, the German police had gone from house to house on Staszic Street to arrest all men, including Uncle Jerzy. I tried to comfort her by saying he'd be back in a few days, but I went home feeling sad. I told Mother, but did not inform Grandma or Grandpa.

Mother immediately went to the prison at Lontski Street and

learned that the men had been taken out of town. A few days went by without any news. Uncle Jerzy never came back.

Because Mother had heard that Dr. Kurzrok was going to open a Jewish hospital, she went to see him, and was appointed director of the new hospital on Alembek Street. She was the very first member of staff to be appointed.

The hospital building had been a school before the war. Beds were brought over from the burnt-out prison. Every day, I would accompany Mother to work and would go and see her there in the evenings.

One day, a high school teacher called Professor P. came to our house informing us that he had news from Father. Prof. P. was tall and thin with a small moustache and black hair. I wanted to run and fetch Mother straight away but Professor P. said we should go to Mrs. Levin's house on Kollontai Street. I rushed over to Mother and we went to Mrs. Levin's house.

When we arrived, Professor P. was already there and was drinking vodka together with another Jewish man. They poured Mother a drink but she didn't want to get drunk, so she discreetly poured the vodka on the floor.

Professor P. told Mother that he knew from Archbishop Szeptycki that Father and Rabbi Levin were alive. He promised that if she and Mrs. Levin would each give 3,000 zlotys, they would get their husband's signature as proof. Mrs. Levin agreed and, a week later, received a cigarette box with her husband's signature on it.

Mother, however, was cautious, and went to ask Mr. Rotfeld for advice. He told her, "If your husband is in Lvov with the Gestapo, he'll come back to you. The committee can buy him out of there. But he isn't in Lvov and Mr. Levin isn't alive, that much I know for sure."

Mother asked if she should demand that they give her the nickname Father used to call me. That was something they couldn't forge because they didn't know it, and that's exactly what she did. They were supposed to bring her the answer a week later. A month went by but Professor P. and the other Jewish man never came back.

In the meantime, Dr. Kurzrok had opened a second hospital at 5 Kursiewicz Street, very close to our house, and Mother was given the position of director. However, it was too hard for her, and she became a secretary there instead. Mr. Labiner was appointed the new director.

Mother had another brother who lived in Niemirow, an urban settlement near Rawa Ruska, a town bordering Ukraine. He had two daughters. Lusia was fourteen and the younger, Roma, was eight. Uncle was a dentist. Every week, he would send us a food parcel.

Gradually the city of Lvov calmed down again, but there were major changes; there were tram cars with "Only for Jews" written in German on them. A Jewish police force was also set up.

Mamoushia wanted me to continue to study. I was now ten years old, and went to class three times a week. There was a group of us: Cesia Kolin, Alma Zellermaier, Alma Jolles, Kuba Liebes, and myself. Every two weeks our place of study changed. Mrs. Wasserman was our teacher.

Cesia's father was working on building some barracks in Janowska Street. One day, after work, they didn't allow him to go home so he had to stay and sleep with the other workers in the barracks they had built. They were told to remove their armbands and were made to wear yellow triangles on the front and back of their clothing. Cesia was crying. She brought packages to her father every day, and stopped coming to class.

A signpost appeared above the entrance to the barracks: *Zwangsarbeitlager*. That's when men started getting hauled off to the camp. The conditions were very bad, and they got beaten mercilessly. People looked like the living dead, like walking skeletons.

Winter was coming. Dr. Kurzrok set up a second hospital for infectious diseases for the prisoners in the camp. The hospital in Alembek Street was moved to Kusciewicz Street. Mamoushia's work was now just a few steps away from home.

3 THE JEWISH QUARTER

Aktions against old people had started. Mamoushia took Grandma and Grandpa with her to her work at the hospital. It was very cold there. They started throwing people out of their flats if they lived outside of the Jewish Quarter. Auntie Sala lived with us now. She brought some coal with her, so it was warm at home.

Dr. Joseph Parnas, the President of the *Judenrat*, got arrested since he refused to cooperate. He was taken to Pelczynska Street and was executed. Now Rotfeld was the President and Landesberg was his Vice-President.

Jews were no longer allowed to pass under the bridge on Zamarstynowska Street. They were only allowed under the bridge on Peltewna Street. The *Schupo* (*Schutzpolizei*) were posted there and would arrest anybody they didn't like. That bridge got nicknamed "Death Bridge".

Alma Zellermayer, who lived opposite us, and I were the only two girls left in class. Mrs. Wasserman had a sister who worked at the hospital and could lend her a health worker armband so that she could come to us. Because of that we were able to continue our education.

It was awfully cold outside. On Sundays, Mother didn't usually work but now she, along with other hospital workers, had to clear away the snow from the city streets.

Dr. Kurzrok and Labiner marched out in front; Kurzrok's wife, a very beautiful woman, was there too. Those who didn't show up to clear away the snow would get fired. Uncle Mundek got frostbite on his feet and Gustak got second degree burns on his hands and feet, so he was exempted from snow duty.

Jacob Hirsch, Mother's cousin, was forced to leave his flat. On the Sunday when he should have been clearing away snow, he was busy packing so he couldn't help. He was fired. While he was running around looking for another job, all of his belongings were stolen leaving him with only with the clothes he had on. Fortunately, he found a job washing bottles at *Rohstoff*, a garbage recycling company.

It was Christmas time and Aunt Marysia invited me to stay at her house for some time. In order not to embarrass her, I went to visit her without my armband, although an order had been given requiring everyone above ten years old to wear one. Visiting her was an opportunity to eat as much as I wanted and also to play.

I only got back home on January 2nd, my eleventh birthday. My family were happy to see me. Aunt Sala baked a cake, Uncle Leon sent me some Niemirov books and Mamoushia bought me a bar of chocolate. January 11th was Mamoushia's birthday. She was ill and was exempt from snow duty. Aunt Sala again baked a big cake, and I brought it to her in bed, dressed in white pyjamas and a white apron, dancing, cake in hand, to *The Little Cook*.

Uncle Mundek was thrown out of his flat together with his children, Gustak and Klara, as well as his second wife, Rena Blumenthal. They all came to live with us. They lived in one of the rooms and the kitchen with Grandpa and Grandma. Mamoushia and I, Aunt Sala and Uncle Hirsch lived in the other room. We had a small oven and Aunt Sala cooked for us.

The flat was in a terrible mess. Since there wasn't enough room for everything, we moved some things down to the cellar. Gustak couldn't stand his stepmother Rena and would sometimes fight with her. Rena in turn refused to cook for him. The truth is that none of us wanted to take care of the poor boy, who was mentally ill.

One day, he took away all his sister's dresses and sold them. Klara understood why he did it and didn't reproach him. When Rena wasn't home, he would come to our room and we would give him something to eat. His sister would also feed him when no one was looking. Sometimes, the poor boy had attacks and would start shouting and hitting things. There was nothing to be done. For Jews there was no Kulparkow, an institute for psychiatric patients, and if we'd declared him sick, he would have been shot. After a fit, he would calm down and say sorry.

They started firing people from their jobs, while simultaneously carrying out *Aktions*. The unemployed were herded into the school near Podzamcze and from there they would get sent to the Belzec concentration camp.

People got fired from their jobs in the following manner: Everyone received a *Meldekarte* — a registration card from the *Arbeitsamt* or Jewish labour office. Every person with a job was allowed to have one additional person at home to run the household. The *Arbeitsamt* would give the worker a *Haushalt* certificate and an armband for that person with the *Meldekarte* number on it and the letter A. Anyone who did not have such a card was deported.

After Uncle Hirsch managed to get Grandpa a job at *Rohstoff* in exchange for money, Grandpa received a *Meldekarte* and an armband. Grandma had a *Haushalt* certificate from Mamoushia and Grandpa. Klara had one from Gustak, her father, and Rena. Aunt Sala had one from Uncle Hirsch.

The President of the *Judenrat*, Mr. Rotfeld, fell ill and died. Mr. Landsberg took over as head of the Committee. Every week, a Jewish newspaper, published in Cracow, was brought to Lvov.

Spring came around, followed by summer. It was 1942. I was studying with Alma, and we became friends. I had another friend, Stenia Wildman. The three of us went for long walks to Holosek, a small town near Lvov. We would save the bread our parents had given us for breakfast and give it to the prisoners from the camp who had to break up tombstones at the Jewish cemetery.

Once an *Askar*, a Ukrainian guard, stopped us because he had seen us give the bread to the prisoners and wanted to take us to the camp because what we had done was forbidden. Fortunately, Stenia had also brought along some tobacco which she gave to the *Askar*. This bribe was accepted, and he let us go.

Care packages were sometimes forwarded to us by the Jewish Committee. One day, Mother received a summons from the Red Cross and we went there together.

It appeared that a parcel from Switzerland had arrived for us. Some time afterwards, we received a parcel from Portugal. We were delighted with the sardines, the condensed milk and the figs but even more so by the fact that somebody had thought of us. There was no information about the sender.

One day, Mamoushia fell ill. She found it hard to breathe. Although it was 11 o'clock at night and Jews were not allowed to be out at that time, I ran to the hospital. It turned out that the doctor on duty was having a drink with Dr. Kurzrok, so I had to go back home alone.

In the morning, I wanted to give Mamoushia the thermometer, but it fell out of my hands and broke. When Mamoushia looked for another thermometer in my night table drawer, she discovered that it was full of bread. It made her really sad and I got a huge telling off. From then on, I no longer supplied bread to the prisoners in the camp.

Yet another levy was demanded from the Jewish community. This time it was seven million in five days. Mother had to spend night and day collecting the money. Some were worried because they had to pay. Others were delighted, thinking that in exchange they would be left in peace.

Two days into collecting the money, Mother received a message from the *Judenrat* informing her that her brother, Leon Blumenthal, his wife and his children had been sent to the Belzec concentration camp. Mother understood that she had to save their lives, so she called the *Judenrat*. An *Aktion* had been carried out in their area. Grandma began to cry.

Mother went to the *Gesundheitskammer* to her friend Blaustein, the Director, who promised to take action. He turned to his German Director who called Rawa Ruska, only to be told that they didn't need a Jewish dentist.

The levy was handed over on Saturday. On Monday at 5 o'clock in the morning we were woken up by gunshots. Mother got up immediately and started waking everybody. Uncle Hirsch went straight to work and Mother and I, together with Grandpa and Grandma, went to the hospital. Gustak went to the Committee and Rena to the Schwarz factory while Uncle Mundek, Klara, and Sala stayed at home.

4 THE 'GREAT AKTION' OF AUGUST 1942

Another *Aktion* began. The *Schupo* and the SS together with the Ukrainian police went from house to house. Cries and screams could be heard all the way to the hospital. People whose relatives had been taken away came to ask Dr. Kurzrok to save them, which he tried to do.

When he got back, Kurzrok announced that the *Arbeitsamt* had been dissolved and that all Jewish matters would from now on be dealt with by the SS. All those in employment had to hand over their *Meldekarten* to be stamped again. Any employee whose card was not stamped would be fired. The *Haushalt* certificates, which were held by a person working for the army, would get stamped at the hospital with a hospital stamp. The *Meldekarten* were handed over to get stamped in the afternoon, and in the meantime, the hospital office issued permits confirming the certificates had been handed in.

Grandpa gave his certificate to Uncle Hirsch. In the meantime, Mamoushia forged a hospital permit and Mr. Labiner signed it.

In the evening, Uncle Hirsch came back with his certificate signed but without Grandpa's certificate. He said that getting Grandpa's certificate signed would cost 5,000. Mother agreed to pay immediately.

Night fell. People slept on the chairs and tables in the hospital office. Grandpa and Grandma slept in the infirmary.

The next day, trucks rolled up to the hospital. Mother removed her white apron and gave it to Grandpa. Suddenly doctors burst into the infirmary shouting, "Run away! Try and save yourselves! We can't help you!"

Grandpa and Grandma ran towards the stairs. But Grandpa soon returned without the apron. He wrote a few words on a piece of paper, pulled out his wallet and handed it, together with the paper, to Dr. Mehrer, asking him to give them to Mother. Grandma managed to get to a storage room where somebody shoved a needle and thread into her hands so she could pretend she was repairing mattresses.

The Germans burst into the office, and shouted to get up. When they scanned the room they noticed me and another little girl. I was next to Mother, who was the only one without an apron.

"*Komm!*" they ordered, and one of the Germans hit me with a wooden leg. Mamoushia pointed at me saying, "That is my child," but she was ignored. The little girl and I left the building. Workers were loading patients onto trucks. One of them recognised Mother and pointed at her saying, "This is a hospital staff member." The German hit him and asked Mother if she had a certificate. From her handbag Mother pulled out a certificate from the Ministry of Health.

Once the Germans had left, Mrs. Redil, the typist, threw her arms around Mother's neck and gave her a hug. Meanwhile, the Jewish police and the hospital staff continued to load patients onto the trucks.

While we were outside, the Germans had burst into the infirmary where they found Grandpa, and took him with them. He stayed quiet and didn't protest, having transmitted his last wishes to Mother through Dr. Mehrer.

Mother was very nervous and only calmed down when we went back inside. When we entered the building, Dr. Mehrer approached us to hand Mother a small package without saying a word. Mother was convinced that Grandpa and Grandma would be safe because the pocket of the apron she had given Grandpa contained two certificates.

It was only in the afternoon when she opened the package, that she understood what happened and burst into tears. In the evening, when Uncle Hirsch came back from work, he brought the stamped registration certificate for Grandpa with him. Unfortunately, it arrived too late.

The *Aktion* went on all week. On Wednesday, they took Aunt Sala. On Saturday, things calmed down a bit and on Sunday we were able to go home with Grandma.

We found out that Uncle Mundek had spent the entire week behind the half open bathroom door and that Klara had been on the other side of the building in the other bathroom. Gustak had been hiding in a pile of trash. Fortunately, they were safe.

On Monday, yet another *Aktion* started. People slept on hospital bed mattresses. A kitchen worker on the ward, a hysterical woman called Kudyszowa, would wake up at night screaming, "There are cars next to the hospital!" The first night, we got really scared of her screaming, but after some time we managed to ignore it.

Kurzrok brought some more signed registration certificates. This time, Mother had one too.

Unexpectedly, my temperature rose to 39.8°. Mother put me in a bed that had been slept in by a patient. The next day, she found two fleas in my pyjamas. My temperature didn't go down.

The *Aktion* continued. Through the hospital windows we could see our block of flats and when they got to our street, Mamoushia looked to see if either her brother or Gustak or Klara had been discovered. She noticed how people's belongings were pillaged by ten-year-old boys who were carrying out dresses, coats and shoes through the gate. She saw Klara being taken away.

It got quiet again on Saturday and we wanted to go home again on Sunday. My temperature still hadn't gone down.

During the previous night, Kudyszowa had woken up screaming "Cars next to the hospital" again, but we didn't pay any attention to her, since we were used to it. Five minutes later, though, we heard men shouting in the corridor, "*Heraus, heraus!*" (Get out, get out!).

Mother dressed me very quickly and a few minutes later we were lined up against the hospital wall while the Germans checked all registration certificates.

We couldn't see Grandma. She wasn't among those lined up against the hospital wall. When Mother wanted to run to the infirmary, Mrs. Redil stopped her, saying, "A daughter is more important than a mother."

Then, the Germans started sorting people. They separated Dr.

Yurim from his son, but since they did not want to leave him, he and his wife went along with their son voluntarily. They took Yanka Glasgal's mother and she followed. Those who remained were taken into the courtyard and orders were given: "On the ground! Get up!" And finally, "Get to work!"

In the kitchen, they started cooking breakfast for the Germans. About an hour later, Landesberg arrived and declared the *Aktion* to be over. An announcement had been made that the ghetto would be closed on the 7th of September.

We went back to an empty house, but physically, I felt better.

The next day, Aunt Reis, my aunt on my father's side, visited us together with her husband and asked whether she could live with us. They were followed by the clerk, Brat and his wife, who had the same request. He was a friend of Father's from when both of them worked for the newspaper. We agreed that even Mrs. Redilova and her mother could live with us.

Brat worked for the *Wohnungsamt* (Housing Authority) and was supposed to get an "order" for a permit for a flat in our building. When the "order" was ready, a hairdresser arrived accompanied by another person with another "order". They started having a row. Since the hairdresser was barber to Ulrich, the commander of Lvov, he got the room.

5 ON THE ARYAN SIDE

Aunt Reis told Mamoushia that she would be able to get me out of the ghetto, over to the Aryan side. Mamoushia asked her how this would be done, and where exactly I would be taken. Aunt Reis informed her that Bobak, a friend of the brother of Aunt Reis's cleaner, Jozia Twardowska, could get me out of the ghetto. Bobak came from Stary Sacz, and would take me from there to his village.

If I had the right papers, it could all be arranged. Mother needed to obtain forged papers for me, and she would need to pay Jozia Twardowska through Aunt Reis. The housekeeper would the money to her brother who would give it to Bobak in regular instalments. Mother agreed to this arrangement since she was well aware of the kind of future that would await me in the ghetto.

In order to get the necessary papers, I went to Aunt Marysia. Much to my dismay, she categorically refused to provide me with a birth certificate or any other kind of forged paperwork.

She was only willing to give me a school certificate from the Russian era that had belonged to Lala, her younger daughter. In the end, Mother somehow managed to obtain a forged birth certificate, in exchange for money.

I was still in the ghetto when Landesberg, along with eleven members of the Jewish police, were hanged. This took place opposite our house at 15 Jaakova Hermana Street on the corner of Lokaitka, where the headquarters of the *Judenrath* could be found.

There was a lot of uncertainty about where I would be taken. I first spent a couple of days at Aunt Reis's house where Mamoushia came to see me. According to Aunt Reis, I was supposed to go to Stary Sacz – as discussed – but Jozia said that Rytro was the destination, and Bobak was thinking of Czarny Potok. So, when I eventually left, Mother didn't know where I would be going.

The place I was taken turned out to be Czarny Potok. As promised, Bobak accompanied me, but he wanted to go back straight away after delivering me. I didn't know why, and he didn't give me an explanation.

In the rural village of Czarny Potok, I would get up very early every morning and go to see the animals. When a cow escaped one day, I ran after her and hurt my leg.

I missed Mamoushia very much and when I was alone, I would cry. She did not know where I was. I had promised her that as soon as I got to my destination I would send her a postcard. I had indeed written one and had given it to Bobak to put in the letter box at the post office while he was there on an errand. A few days after he got back, I found out that he hadn't posted my card after all.

During this time, Mother had heard no news from me and was understandably very worried. Aunt Reis and her husband had run away, and Jozia and her brother were refusing to speak to Mother who did not trust them.

Because of her worries and the nagging uncertainty, Mother became ill. In addition, she had problems with her flat, with her work at the hospital and also with her brother Mundek, who had stopped working for the Jewish Committee.

Thanks to some connections and through payment, Mother was able to get her brother a job in the ghetto sewers. The commander of the ghetto was now a German called Mansfeld and the workers in the ghetto were called "Mansfelders". So, Mundek became a Mansfelder.

Mrs. Bronia Brat, who recognised Mother's problems, promised to help. She managed to send someone she knew, Mrs. Stasia Magierowska, to bring me to Rytro, a village about 83 kilometres south-east of Cracow. It was too unsafe in Lvov.

The brother of Aunt Reis's cleaner, Twardowska, had once lived in Rytro, and we had visited Twardowska there once with Bobak. Mrs. Stasia somehow obtained my address in Czarny Potok, and walked all the way to find me. Bobak was very surprised.

By September 20th 1942, I was back in Lvov because I had been badly treated in the countryside. I was temporarily staying on the Aryan side with Mrs. Stasia and her mother at 12 Hoffman Street.

Mother still worked at the hospital, and Gustak still worked as a messenger boy for the Jewish Council, while Uncle Mundek was working in the sewers and Uncle Hirsch was collecting bottles outside the ghetto. Once a week, I would go and see Uncle Hirsch at 21 Kazimierzowska Street, where he worked, and every week Mother would come and see me.

There were rumours now that people would be moved into barracks. This news made people very scared. I begged Mother to take steps to protect herself and she began to do so.

Mrs. Yadzia Piotrowska managed to get Mother papers stating she was a Christian, and was also supposed to rent a room for her outside the ghetto, where Mother would try to find work as a Polish woman. My school friend Hela Gangel had taken refuge with Mrs. Yadjia, a friend of Mother's. Sometimes Hela and I would go for a walk together and take Mrs. Piotrowska's children with us.

One day a woman I didn't know came to the house and asked to speak with me. I thought Mrs. Yadzia had sent her. She said, "I work for the Gestapo. Your name is Janina Hescheles and not Lidia Wereszczynska. If you don't give me 5,000 zlotys by 4 o'clock this afternoon, then it'll be off to Piaski with you[1]!"

I ran to Uncle, who immediately informed Mamoushia, who came at four. The woman turned up and they had a discussion. Mother knew it was blackmail so they haggled, and in the end the woman accepted only 100 zlotys.

In the ghetto, the process of turning sleeping quarters into barracks had begun and people were really afraid of what was going to happen. Mother didn't want to bring me back to the ghetto. I was supposed to stay a few more days with Mother's friend, Mrs. Stasia Magierowska, until Mother found an alternative. Under these uncertain circumstances, she couldn't think about her own safety.

On the following Tuesday, a woman unknown to me came to the house and found me in the kitchen. She warned me about a visit from the Gestapo. I immediately told Mother this alarming news.

Since there was no time to hesitate, I was swiftly relocated to 11 Kasper Boczkowski Street where an acquaintance of Mrs. Stasia's mother lived. She was called Kordybowa and was a 60-year-old woman who tried to look 35 and introduced her husband as her father. In the mornings, she wandered around Solski Square (Black Market Square) and spent her afternoons playing cards.

Meanwhile Dr. Kurzrok set up a camp hospital on Janowska Street and came to the ghetto twice a week. On other days, Dr. Tadanier, his deputy, filled in for him at the ghetto hospital. Dr. Tadanier's wife, son, and daughter were on the Aryan side.

Another *Aktion* took place in the ghetto, which was now completely closed off. Jews had to march to work in columns of three. Each division was clearly marked with the letters W (*Wehrmacht*, Army) or R (*Rüstung*, Armament). Registration certificates were no longer valid. The *Judenrat* was disbanded, and its salaried workers were killed in Piaski. Only a certain number of people were transferred to the camp.

Gustak was transferred to the camp and was assigned to the *Reinigung* (the cleaners) section. Uncle Hirsch got a W. I would run to him every day. From him I got the sad news that Aunt Reis and her husband had been betrayed and were no longer alive.

Uncle Mundek had caught typhus and it was unclear whether he still lived because with every *Aktion*, trucks arrived at the hospital to pick up patients. Rena was already in the barracks and wore the letter R. Mamoushia didn't have an R or a W, but the hospital was given two buildings for its workers to use as barracks at 3 and 5 Szaraniewicz Street.

The *Aktion* was largely over. Only Jewish police continued and the people they caught were transferred to the prison at 12 Waisenhof Street. Every other Saturday, the prisoners were transferred to Piaski and killed.

Uncle Mundek got better and moved to the barracks. Mamoushia did too. I missed her so much. Kordybowa beat me a lot and I was really unhappy there. Sometimes, she wouldn't even give me anything to eat. I didn't tell Mamoushia because I didn't want to make her sad. The unhappier I got, the more I missed Mother. I decided to run away from Kordybowa and go to the barracks.

Ever since the ghetto had been turned into barracks, it was known as the *Julag, Jüdischer Arbeitslager*, a Jewish work camp. Kordybowa found out that I wanted to flee, so she beat me. She said that if I missed my mother so much, she should come to us here so we could be together. Mother hesitated, afraid that it could harm both of us. On the other hand, she felt sorry for me and decided to come – she told me she had no money and that Uncle Hirsch would pay for us. Mamoushia arrived. Uncle Hirsch was supposed to bring Mother's things gradually over a few days, not all in one go. He would bring them to his work and then Kordybowa was supposed to bring them over to us from there.

The head of the *Julag* was a German called Grzymek and his deputy was called Heinisch. The *Judenrat* had been dismantled, but there was an *Unterkunft* – a German administration office that ran the *Julag*. Every day before setting off to work, there was an assembly attended by Grzymek and Heinisch. You had to be very careful, if you were carrying anything noticeable you would have it taken away and get sent to the Waisenhof prison or the camp as a punishment. Since the Germans were posted at the main gate, Uncle Hirsch only brought a few items with him each day. Every few days, I would go and collect them. Uncle told me that W letters had been handed out to people at the hospital and that Kurzrok's deputy, Dr. Tadanier, had escaped but had later been caught and was in Waisenhof with his wife and son. The hospital workers were collecting money to have him freed.

6 THE ARREST

Kordybowa hadn't been to "Black Market Square" for a few days and was about to do her shopping. She took some money from Mother and left. First, she went to Uncle Hirsch. Uncle and several workers had asked her to buy something so they had given her some money.

Uncle Hirsch and a few other workers had gone to pick up a shipment of bottles that day. While passing through Smolki Square, where the headquarters of the *Schutzpolizei* was located, he noticed Kordybowa who was just leaving the building. He didn't ask what she had been doing there.

An hour later, after returning to his workplace, he found Kordybowa in tears. There had been a raid, she said, and she had lost all her money while trying to get away. Uncle Hirsch was very concerned when he heard this story, it made him fear for our safety. He asked Kordybowa to let me visit him the next day. I went to him and he was very glad, believing that his fears had been unjustified, and did not tell me anything. I returned home.

When someone came to Kordybowa's apartment, the arrangement was that Mother would hide inside the closet. I myself was officially registered as Kordybowa's niece, an orphan.

On Tuesday, Kordybowa emptied a closet in another room and said that Mother should hide in there. I came back from seeing Uncle, took off my coat, went to the second room and sat down next to Mother by the stove. I was very happy to be with her and asked her to tell me what she would do on the day after the war ended. We daydreamed aloud, but I doubted whether any of these dreams could ever be realised.

A knock on the door put an end to our daydreaming. Mother quickly hid inside the closet and I went to the kitchen. Kordybowa opened the front door and three policemen from the *Schupo* entered, one of them shouting "Who lives here?" Kordybowa pointed to her husband and me. They entered the room and ordered to have the light switched on.

Since we had no electricity in the apartment, I wanted to go to the kitchen to fetch some matches. One of the policemen took hold of me, slapped me, then took his rifle and struck me in the back with the butt.

They opened the closet in which Kordybowa had wanted Mother to hide, and continued their search. They pushed open the other closet, pulled out Mother, and beat her with their rifle butts.

Then they shouted in Polish, "Hands up and face the wall," and started searching her. They found two vials of cyanide in the muffs of her coat sleeves.

One of them asked, "What do you need this for, Jew?" Without waiting for a reply, he kicked her. Mother fainted and fell. One of them shouted, "Housewife! Bring water. Your Jew-woman has fainted!"

Then they searched us and the apartment, but when they only found 1,500 zlotys in Mother's handbag, they shouted, "Where's the money?" We didn't tell them, and they found nothing.

They ordered us to pack all our belongings into a single bundle, to get dressed and to put the bundle on our backs, and then they led us to Smolki Square.

We sat there on a bench for about an hour. They asked us how long we had been living in Kordybowa's apartment on the Aryan side and were surprised that Mother had done such a thing when she had a job. Mother whispered to me that if they sent us to the Waisenhof prison there was still a chance of doing something, but if they brought us to the Gestapo in Pełczyńska Street, they would send us straight to Piaski.

An hour later we were transported to Pełczyńska Street while two policemen marched beside us, and one behind. On the way, Mother reproached herself for not having taken me back to the ghetto. I consoled her by saying that she was in no way responsible. She had done everything she could and was prepared to sacrifice herself for me. We couldn't imagine that we would end up like this because of Kordybowa. I took the blame. Mother could have gone to Jadzia Piotrowska if she didn't have problems with me, but ultimately we had to accept that this was our destiny.

At the Gestapo, they brought us into a small room in which three Germans were seated. They ordered us to turn to the wall and raise our hands. Fortunately, there were no beatings this time, but we had to stand with our hands up for a long time. A Pole, who was translating, apparently knew Father and managed to save us from imprisonment in Pełczyńska.

Even though it was ice cold outside, it was stifling in the little room where we were kept. I whispered to Mother that I would faint if I had to stand any longer. She asked permission for me to sit on the floor. They let me.

At 8 o'clock, the translator and one of the Germans left the room, and they offered me a chair. Mother continued to stand up. The two remaining Germans placed a radio with an English language programme before us. Another German left and the remaining German offered Mother a chair, too, and picked up the phone: "*Jüdischer Ordnungsdienst?*" (The Jewish militia). Upon hearing these words, Mother was relieved.

At 1 o'clock that night we were in the *Julag*. There, Mother saw the editor Brat. They took us to the prison on Waisenhof Street, and into a tiny cell in which there were about 60 people packed together – sitting on one another, men, women and children. When we entered the cell, someone in the corner remarked, "Another herring to be pickled," and someone near the door added, "In fact, two herrings!" Mother didn't allow me to lie down on the floor because it disgusted her. We remained standing for one day and one night. In the morning women from the kitchen brought us coffee.

The ghetto community paid for food for the prisoners, but we were not hungry; neither Mother nor I could swallow a thing. The cell was stifling because of the sweat and the stench, even though it was the 22nd of February. In the corner, there were some leaking buckets into which both men and women relieved themselves. Whoever had a useful acquaintance, or whoever paid 100 zlotys, was allowed to go into the courtyard.

On Wednesday, I drank some coffee but was unable to stand any longer on my legs. Although Mother didn't permit me to lie down, for fear of me getting lice, I said "May God permit me to contract typhus, but I doubt whether I'll have such luck," and I lay down. Mother also wanted to lie down, but there was no space. So, she lay down in my place and I lay on top of her.

In the morning, they counted us and the women were then transferred to a cell for women only. In that cell there were about 100 women with crying children and, due to a lack of space, they were lying on top of each other. Mr. Brat and Uncle Hirsch intervened on our behalf before Forschirer and Hasenus, the commanders of the prison. As a result, they transferred us to another cell where we met Dr. Tadanier.

We wanted to be deported as soon as possible, because waiting was torture. Finally, the day before our deportation arrived. On Friday, one of the commanders, Hasenus, entered the cell, called out the names of Dr. Tadanier and his wife and son, picked several young and pretty girls, and took them with him.

We understood that we were lost. I could no longer control myself and started to cry. We were not so much afraid of dying, but of the possibility that children would but be buried alive. Some prayed to be hit by an accurate shot, others sang the national anthem, *Hatikvah*, in Hebrew. Mother tried to comfort me and promised to cover my eyes when they started to shoot. I calmed down and joined those singing.

At three in the morning a policeman entered the cell and called Mother's name. Mother went to the door. He asked whether she had a child with her and both of us went out into the corridor. Forschirer was waiting for us and led us to a cell that could be entered from the courtyard. Dr. Tadanier and the others who had been taken out with him by Hasenus were there. Here there was no bucket, for lack of space, and no one was allowed into the courtyard. It was not permitted to talk aloud, nor to sneeze. We were still not saved.

On Saturday, at 7 o'clock in the morning, the first car arrived. After the car left again, they opened our cell and in groups of five they put us in a cellar. Now, and only now, could we be considered "saved". Erich Engels, the head of the Department of Jewish Affairs in the Lvov ghetto, arrived, read out several names, among them ours, and the policeman said that we were in the first transport. Several men were sent to the Janowski camp.

The evacuation was carried out as follows: Policemen would open all the cells. The *Sonderdienst*, men of the Special Service composed of Poles, Ukrainians and Germans, whose duty it was to carry out special tasks, would enter the cells shouting *"Heraus! Heraus!"* and beat the prisoners with the butts of their rifles. More than 40 prisoners were forced to climb onto a truck and lie on top of each other, with members of the *Sonderdienst* standing in each corner with rifles drawn over the prisoners.

After all the trucks had left, they transferred us to a cell and every two hours they freed a couple of people into the *Julag*.

When I was taken outside and breathed the fresh air, I felt as though I was drunk.

7 BACK TO THE GHETTO

In the barracks of the *Julag* at 5 Szaraniewicze Street, I washed myself thoroughly and put on Mother's underwear. Mother hung up our coats to be aired while Ms. Bronia prepared lunch for us. Uncle Hirsch returned from work in the afternoon, was happy to see us, and told us that on Thursday Kordybowa had come to see him and had demanded Mother's clothes. He couldn't control himself and gave her a dressing-down.

In the evening, Mother went to the hospital and got her job back. She bought herself the letter W and obtained typhus immunisation injections for both of us. After the third injection, however, I got a fever, my arm got swollen and my head ached. My temperature didn't go down for three days on end, but Mother didn't want to take me to the hospital. During five days I had a fever and on the sixth day a rash appeared, a clear sign of the illness. I didn't have the strength to stand up and I had to be taken to hospital after all.

It was a question of "Out of the frying pan into the fire". I stayed at the hospital for a week, semi-conscious, and then they came to evacuate the patients. Mother dressed me, but instead of taking me to the truck, she took me to the infirmary and covered me with a white laboratory coat. While I was in hospital Mrs. Tadanier occupied the bed next to me. Oleś, her son, had also contracted typhus, but had somewhat recovered and frequently visited his mother. Dr. Tadanier had died of the illness.

Mother sat by my bed every day for some six hours. After four days, she contracted a fever herself. When the doctor examined her, he diagnosed typhus. From then on, she lay next to me. After a few days her fever fortunately came down.

Until now, Mother had never caught typhus, but after staying for so long in the ward for infectious diseases, it was to be expected. Rena, too, came down with typhus and gangrene in her feet. There was hope that it would only be necessary to amputate the toes of her feet, but they took her away when evacuating the other patients. We never saw her again.

One night, members of the *Sonderdienst* surrounded the barracks of the Mansfeld workers and transported 50 men to Żółkiew, where they were obliged to dig trenches. Some 40 were taken to the Janowski camp. Uncle Mundek was among the 50 taken to Żółkiew, and he was shot there. Then they began to 'contract' the *Julag*; part of its population was killed. A hospital was closed, and the employees were concentrated in the opposite building.

In May I worked in the hospital garden. We were indifferent to our work because we knew we would never harvest the fruit of our labour. I played with Oleś, Maryśka Marksamer, and Henryk Weiner. One day Henryk fled from the *Julag* with his mother.

Preparations for the liquidation of the *Julag* had begun. Women who worked in the D.A.W. (*Deutsche Ausrüstungswerke*, factories that were part of the German Armaments Works, a division of the SS) were transferred to spend the night at work. As part of the liquidation of the *Julag*, Uncle Hirsch was supposed to move to the Janowska camp.

The day before the liquidation of the ghetto arrived. Mother told me to go to Aunt Marysia. That was on the Monday. I left the ghetto in a column of Rohstoff workers at 6 in the morning.

On the way, I escaped from the column and ran away as fast as I could. I went to the door on the side of the garden. It was locked. I knocked, but nobody opened. I climbed over the railings and knocked on the window of Aunt Marysia's house. Through it I saw Irka, Lala, and their mother in their beds. Aunt Marysia was reading a newspaper. When she heard me knocking, she looked towards the window and saw me, but turned to her newspaper again and didn't move from the bed to open the door. I stood there for another few moments, returned and knocked again on the door, but nobody opened it.

I then decided to go to Uncle Hirsch. The other bottle store was surrounded by Ukrainian police and Uncle advised me to run back and sneak into the *Julag* through the opening in the fence. So, I returned to the place I had tried to escape from. I saw a column of people from the night shift at Schwarz (a textile workshop) returning to the *Julag* and I entered together with them. At 10 o'clock I was already in the hospital. I greeted Mother with a smile. When Bronia Brat saw me, she nearly fainted.

8 SEPARATION FROM MOTHER

That night Mother couldn't sleep. On Tuesday morning, we intended to go down to the shelter in the hospital since another *Aktion* appeared to coming up. The hidden entrance was through the chimney of the movable kitchen stove in the apartment of Mr. Labiner. In the afternoon Dr. Kurzrok arrived. From the *Julag* he collected his father, his cousin, Ms. Adlersberg, and Mr. Labiner with his wife and son and went with them to the camp hospital. The Labiner family then travelled on to Cracow. Uncle did not return from work but had also not returned to collect his belongings in the camp.

Mother lay in her bed; she was very pale. I lay down beside her and asked, "Why are you so sad? There is still no *Aktion*." Mother answered, "For me it has already begun and, even though I have cyanide pills, my death will be very hard for me, because of you. What will become of me doesn't bother me for a minute," she burst out, crying bitterly. "Janola, save me this last agony and leave me, I don't want to know what happens to you, I don't want to see you next to me! Go now if you love me. Go back to that woman. The humiliation will be mine, because it's me who asks you to go to her."

I didn't want to obey her, and replied, "What is there to live for? In any case, I won't survive without documents. Mother, do you want to prolong my suffering? Won't it be better to finish once and for all, hugging each other? What is life on my own worth to me?"

But Mother pleaded with me. "You must go! You have to avenge me and your father!"

I answered, "Will revenge restore you to me? Is it worth living just for that? Is it worth suffering so much just for that? Wouldn't it be better to finish everything, next to you? Mother, you would save me from so much of the suffering and agony that await me."

Struggling with Mother was difficult for me. I couldn't look at her crying; her face was all wrinkled, just like Grandmother's face. Her heart pounded so loudly that I could hear it.

Finally, I yielded and agreed, on condition that Mother gave me cyanide as a contingency. She refused, gave me 2,700 zlotys for the journey and accompanied me to the gate. She kissed me and we parted from Mr. and Mrs. Brat.

Mother kissed me again and when I was already in the queue to leave the ghetto, she whispered to me, "Bear all suffering bravely for my sake."

I went again to Aunt Marysia. This time the door was open and I entered without knocking. When Auntie saw me, she couldn't throw me out. I gave her part of the money so I could stay at her place.

The liquidation of the *Julag* was coming to an end and after five days Auntie no longer wanted me to remain with her. I went to find Uncle Hirsch, but in the workshop there were no Jews left. I learnt from an Aryan watchman that the workshop had been searched, they had found arms and all the Jewish workers had been executed, among them Uncle Hirsch.

So, I returned to Aunt Marysia, intending to go to the camp hospital the next day. Before I left early in the morning, Aunt took the money from me, saying she would try to do something for me. She gave me two slices of bread and I got back 200 zlotys.

I went to find Kurzrok at the hospital, but he appeared to be no longer alive. Dr. Maksymilian Kurzrok was head of both the ghetto hospital and the Janowski camp hospital. Since his position enabled him to move freely between the two sites, he took the opportunity to bring medicines from the ghetto to the camp.

It was only as the ghetto was about to be liquidated, when his role as a "liaison officer" came to an end, that he decided to escape. He had intended to flee with his wife and some young hospital employees, who planned to join the Polish and Ukrainian brigades working on the defence fortifications at Dnepropetrovsk. But when they were at the railway station, two informers, Pecherz and Szwadron, Jews who worked for the Gestapo, recognised him and reported them[1]. Only seventeen of the hospital staff remained. Kurzrok and his fellow escapees were murdered.

Gustak had been shot when the *Reinigung* unit in the camp was liquidated. In the hospital, I spoke with Ms. Adlersberg who advised me to approach the D.A.W. the following day.

I had no choice but to return to Auntie. The next morning, Auntie found a note on which was written: "Madam! A filthy Jew is staying with you. Produce 20,000 zlotys, or else you'll land up in Piaski together with this filthy person."

I was wondering who had written the note. I had not seen anybody I knew, not on my way to the hospital, nor on my way back. I thought it was likely that Helene Nowicka, a friend of Auntie, had sent the letter at the request of my Aunt. Helene Nowicka, to whom she confided all her problems, was an anti-Semite; during the pogroms she would go out to beat Jews.

When I had parted from her, my Aunt had promised that she would make an effort to find something for me – and if she didn't succeed, she would return the money through Ms. Adlersberg.

9 IN THE D.A.W. AND THE JANOWSKI CAMP

At 117 Janowska Street, there was a knitting shop. At the entrance gate stood a watchman. In order to enter, I had to tell him that I was a Jew. I approached the Jewish supervisor of the workshop, Ms. Bronia Muszkat, and waited for half a day to speak to her. Then, on the D.A.W. grounds, I found Ms. Redil, head of the cutting division. There were barracks which housed 500 women, in which I would be safer than in the camp. Ms. Redil asked a friend of hers, Mr. Schächter, to let me move into the barracks. It was true that I was entitled to do so, as a young girl, but I was advised not to.

Finally, they found me a job as a "finisher" in the sewing shop of what had been the Schwarz factory, in the team headed by Elza Maro and Hanka Weber. Here, not all the women had been transferred to the women's camp, because not all of the barracks were ready, so I slept with them in the workshop.

The workshops were located in long huts with roofs that leaked, with rain coming in between the tiles. The chief of the D.A.W.

was Fritz Gebauer, his assistant was Müller, and there were two sadists who were responsible for "order", Bajer and Melchior.

For every two workshops there was a supervisor (*Aufseher*). Haberowa was the Jewish supervisor of all the sewing shops. There were also many *Zurichter* (those responsible for the preparatory work). Every separate workshop had its own director: Elza Maro, Hanka Weber, Lusia Münzer, Bronia Muszkat, Cyla Morgentraub, Róża Radil, Grinbaum and Kohn.

The workshop was divided up into teams. Each team had its own head, two people who prepared material to be sewn (*Zurichter*), a person who ironed (*Bügler*), twenty people who sewed using sewing machines, and fifteen assistants. Hilferding headed the sewing office and Löbel the technical office.

Administration officials and overseers lived in the barracks. Tusia, sister-in-law of Bronia, was in charge of the women in the barracks. The barracks consisted of four wooden buildings, and one of them housed the washroom and kitchen. In three of the huts with leaking roofs were four-tier bunks reaching up to the ceiling. These bunks were separated by an aisle every nine rows. Only one woman slept in each bunk. Food was distributed in exchange for food vouchers (*Esskarte*). The women used to eat half lying down, since their heads would otherwise hit the bunk above.

Work would start at 6 o'clock in the morning. I was unable to meet the work quota, nor was I able to sit still all the time in one place. Bauerowa, our foreman, sometimes rebuked me, but Elza Maro never said anything to me. I would run around between the workshops on the pretext that I was going to see the doctor, and would arrive at Maks Boruchovicz's[1] packaging workshop.

Two weeks later we were transferred to the women's camp

(*Frauenlager*). In the camp, I was one of the privileged ones. I got to know Akser, who worked in the administration office of the camp and directed the illegal aid network.

Thanks to him I was transferred to the hut of the laundry workers (*Wäscherei*) which was cleaner and not so crowded. I met Orland and was not obliged to stand in the soup queue. Later, thanks to Akser, I could have my lunch together with the laundry workers. We got Saturday afternoons off and in the morning the women always had a shower. The laundry workers had the day off on Sundays.

Elza Maro would free me from the workshop and I would go to the camp offices, to Bronek Jakubowicz[2]. Sometimes Ilian, Grün[3], Fränkel[4], Kleinman[5] and Herman with the accordion would appear and we would entertain ourselves for two hours. At 6 o'clock Franka Stein, from the barracks, would join us and sing.

In the D.A.W. there was also an "Aryan" workshop. The Aryan workers arrived in the morning, at noon they had a break, and at 6 o'clock in the evening they returned home. Among them was Stasia Magierowska.

In the women's camp, we always got up at 3.30 in the morning; at 4.00 we left our area and marched in groups of five towards the men's camp. At the gate of the parade ground of the men's camp there was a basket of bread. The cook gave the woman at the end of each group five slices of bread and she then distributed them.

The orderly (*Ordner*) and a camp policeman (*Lagerpolizist*) kept order. If somebody pushed, they whipped him. Then they distributed coffee, but in order to get some, one had to use force. Most women would forsake this coffee; It was warm but very bitter. Until 5 o'clock we were allowed to chat with the men. Then the camp police would disperse the clusters and order us to stand again in groups of five, according to our sections.

In each column there were 100 prisoners. Those in charge first counted us and then stood in front of their columns. The roll-call began. Warzok, the camp commander (who got this post after Wilhaus was sent to the front), walked between the columns and issued orders such as: "Attention - stand! At ease - stand! Down! Up! Crawl! Jump!" The camp police saw to it that the orders were scrupulously obeyed. Then the orchestra began to play and the columns, one after the other, marched out of the parade ground.

First came those who worked in the town, then columns of women who worked in the D.A.W., and after them the men from the D.A.W. When we passed the security hut (*Kontrolstube*), the heads of the columns would deliver their reports and Akser would record them. Here the medical doctor, Dr. Biber, would wait, as well as the German watchmen (*Wachmänner*). A little further on, the Ukrainian watchmen would gather for their roll-call. Opposite the security hut, the orchestra would play again.

We marched along the wall, passing the "bunker" adjoining the main gate. Through the grating, children and adults (who had been caught on the Aryan side and were held here) would stare enviously at us. Then we would enter the D.A.W. area. Here Kurzer, a German, would receive the written report. Then there was Melchior, who would seize anything a person carried with him, apart from the mess tin and a slice of bread. We would march past the house of Gebauer, who stood before the gate together with the German overseers.

The race to meet the quotas then began: every person with a

machine had to sew four pairs of trousers, jackets or coats. The helpers had to finish the job by adding buttons and buttonholes. If we didn't finish by 6 o'clock, the work continued until 8 o'clock and the next day the whole group was sent to do dirty or heavy manual work, like cleaning latrines or carrying bricks.

Sometimes there was no work to do. We would hold something in our hands, just to give the impression that we were working. The one-and-a-half-hour noon break started at 12.30. Women who lived in the barracks went back to eat a good soup, often with barley or potatoes. We, however, were obliged to go back to the camp. Whoever remained behind in the workshop was punished with twenty-five lashes.

We arranged ourselves into columns, which took about half an hour. Two policemen and two orderlies then accompanied us back to the camp. At the checkpoint, Striks counted us. In the parade ground, two large pots were ready and two young fellows were distributing soup with a ladle. Whoever had "protection" received thicker soup. In the soup there were sometimes two pieces of potato, some oats, and some leaves of kohlrabi or carrot tops floating on the surface. Orland, the chief overseer, with a whip in his hand, saw to it that nobody got two portions.

Then, with all of the other columns, we stood in line at the entrance to the dining room. One after the other, the columns went inside to eat. Five minutes later, we already went outside and arrived at the gate of the D.A.W. Here we waited, since the gate was only opened at 2 o'clock. Again, we'd work under duress; with clothes drenched in sweat. At 6 o'clock work was over and there was roll-call inside the D.A.W.

Exhausted, we dragged ourselves to the camp while the orchestra played outside the offices. The children of the watchmen would listen. The *Askars* played soccer on their own field. We went to the washroom; most women came here to meet acquaintances or to buy something. There were stone troughs and channels, and above them were pipes with cold running water. At the sides were faucets. You had to have "protection" in order to get a wash basin. The men washed after us.

After Orland's whistle, we got into columns and walked to the women's camp. Then it was the men's turn to wash. In the *Frauenlager,* they distributed soup or a slice of bread with a warm liquid called *Lorke* (a bitter plant coffee). Orland was no longer present. Bebi (the Jewish head of the women's camp) would scream, the women orderlies would beat us, but the efforts to impose order were to no avail.

On Mondays, they distributed a spoon of sour beets, sweetened with saccharine, and very infrequently with "honey butter" or spoilt fetid cheese. At 9 o'clock it was "lights out", but it was not quiet until ten. Every night a control was carried out by a different guard (*Wachmann*), and two orderlies were on duty. They didn't sleep. In the morning, they woke up the women in all the huts. During the day, the orderlies cleaned the washroom and the latrines.

The first month in the camp was horrible. Every day when we came back from work, we found children and people from the *Julag* and from the bunkers who had been shot near our latrine. They had been forced to get undressed, fold their clothes and to arrange them in a pile. A delegation from the women's camp requested that the place of execution be moved. It was transferred to the rear of the kitchen. There the bodies lay a few days until there were enough and then they were taken by people of the "death brigade" to be burnt in the sands of Piaski.

The death brigade consisted of strong men, who were chosen from those destined to be executed. Every so often they were replaced. They were separated from us, but we saw them from afar when they were working. They had their own shack in Piaski. At every step, they were accompanied by a German, a member of the SD (*Sicherheitsdienst,* Security Service). They would extract the bodies of people who were killed in August 1942 from the mass graves, to destroy the proof that this had been a place of mass executions. The clothes of the condemned prisoners were stored in warehouses.

An acquaintance of Mother's, Dr. Tanne, worked in the clinic of the D.A.W. He had worked together with Mother in the hospital on Dwernicki Street under the Russians, and in the ghetto hospital on Kuszevicza Street under the Germans. He had been together with Mother and with the editor Brat and his wife Bronia in the bunker of Labiner. They had waited together for execution in the *Frauenlager* when Orland had managed to save him. From the women in the laundry, I learned that the women who had cyanide pills lay down in a circle and poisoned themselves.

The second month passed quietly. Every Friday or Saturday we would go to the bathhouse in Szpitalna Street. The journey there was not pleasant. As we passed through the town, passers-by and children would stare at us. Not wanting them to notice our sorry state, we would sing joyous marching songs.

On Saturday afternoon, we were free. In order to amuse ourselves a little, we organised "evening entertainments", but the awful reality never left us and the songs and the poems we recited spoke for themselves.

At work it was terribly hot, and at night the fleas and the stifling heat did not let us sleep.

After 9 o'clock in the evening it was forbidden to be outside, but the more audacious women would nevertheless go out. I, too, would frequently go out behind the hut and there we would sing and recite poetry. During such nights, many thoughts crossed my mind and I would compose poems which did not rhyme.

From the sands of Piaski, opposite us, embers would fly up from the burning bodies. An unpleasant odor hung in the air. I longed for Mother, but didn't cry. I envied the fact that everything was over for her. I looked in the direction of the fire, in which, even now, she was perhaps going up in flames. I knew that I, too, would be incinerated there... Such thoughts became less and less frequent. I wanted to spend my final moments laughing, but our laughter was artificial.

Every second woman had scabies, an itchy skin infection. At first it was possible to get treated in the hospital, but later people were taken to Piaski together with those in the "cooler" (solitary confinement) who had been caught on the Aryan side. Hospital inmates were taken there, too. It is no wonder women were afraid to ask for help. The hospital was situated at 138 Janowska Street and could be accessed only from the street in the company of *Askars*.

The time came that I could no longer move freely in the *Gelände*, the open space in the D.A.W. in which the men's camp was situated. In the middle of this open space there was a bench on which prisoners were beaten.

Scheisskarte, permits to use the toilets, were issued. If anyone was caught without one, they would get twenty-five lashes of the whip. There were three *Scheisskarte* for every group, one for every fifteen workers in "finishing", one for every twenty who worked on the sewing machines, and the third one for the *Brigadier* (foreman), the *Zurichter* (designer) and the *Bügler* (ironer). We would register for a place in the *Scheisskarte* queue before the foreman. Before the latrine stood an *Ordner*, making sure that no one without a *Scheisskarte* entered. I could no longer take a permit from the group, as it would have caused unpleasantness for my fellow workers since I often used the card to take a break from work. Finally, the foreman, whom I knew, gave me a *Scheisskarte* as a gift.

10   THE HANGING

There were no Germans in front of the gate. Kurzer looked at us with a grim face and we sensed that something bad was about to happen. The work orderlies (*Werkordner*) did not permit us to enter the workshops and all the Germans were *Scheisskarte* stationed in the middle of the *Gelände*. We were alarmed, fearing that there would be a "selection", but instead, the German, Reryk, tied ropes to one of the lampposts. We understood that someone on the night shift was going to be hanged.

The inmates had organised a celebration and everyone had been drinking. The man who was about to be killed had carried a pistol and when he was drunk, had used it. I was all nerves and panicky, but when it transpired that there was to be an execution, I calmed down. I looked indifferently at the man who was undressing. Once I had seen him selling soap and had bought a piece from him.

Now, the German Melchior was explaining to him how to slip

the noose of the rope around his neck. He was calm, as if this was a matter of money or soap. He climbed onto the ramp, wearing only his underwear.

I found his nonchalance jarring. I couldn't bear to see how he calmly slipped the noose around his neck, so I left the ranks, but the *Ordner* ordered me to returned to my place. I went back and looked at the condemned man. He was already hanging, his body convulsing. I again felt agitated, but not out of pity for the man, nor from the staged execution or from fear of death.

The execution only renewed the awareness, that couldn't be dismissed lightly, awareness of a reality that I couldn't accept. This was the first time that I witnessed an execution. The last time I was afraid even to look at the condemned.

I still used to sleep in the workshop. I often went to the women's camp to see Lucy Hasenus, who was an orderly at that time. People from the *Julag* were sitting in the women's camp. The women gave them bread.

At 7 o'clock a German called Siller came for an inspection. He went by the huts, looking at the distribution of coffee. I left the barracks to go to the latrine. On the way to the latrine I saw that people were undressing. I was afraid to go back and afraid to continue. I closed my eyes, nearly stopped breathing, and started to run to the latrine. I was afraid of going back so stayed where I was. Sometimes one had to quarrel for a place. It was no different this time. A woman pushed me and I nearly fell into the latrines.

Then, all of a sudden one could hear shots, and then everything went quiet. Two women were crying. One of them had a son, another a sister in the barracks. I shuddered, unable to control myself. Other women weren't as close as me, but saw everything.

They weren't as afraid as I was. I couldn't eat or sleep. Lucy comforted me, saying, "There's nothing to be done about it, you'll end up the same way. When you move to the women's camp you'll get used to seeing such things."

After the hanging I was no longer afraid of death, not that of somebody else or myself, but under no circumstances could I come to terms with it. I very much wanted to live – to live at all costs. I felt that something inside of me was calling: "Live! Live!" I didn't have the strength to oppose it and I did not succeed in silencing it.

I remembered that once on a Sunday, at Jakubowicz, somebody asked why there were no acts of bravery performed by Jews. Kleinmann answered, "Wasn't it an act of courage, when girls went to Piaski singing, without crying or screaming?" I found this unacceptable. It meant yielding to death, with indifference and acceptance, like the man who was hanged. Is this bravery? Must I be a hero like this? No! I have to live! It is preferable to suffer, to fast, only in order to live, because I love life. If I go to Piaski, then only in order to live. I won't try to run away, but I'll resist the murderers! I won't undress!

One day, Stasia Magierowska approached me. She told me she could help me escape. I needed to obtain a passport photo. She and Ms. Adamska would then send it to Warsaw, and within a week I would obtain a *Kennkarte*, an identity card confirming that I was an Aryan, so I could travel to Warsaw with a certain woman from Brzuchowicze. Flaschner, head of the workshop, took a photo of me in secret. I consulted with Bumek Wahrman[1] from the underground, who would contact Magierowska.

According to Magierowska, this was an offer from a committee concerned with helping people escape. I noticed that a girl,

Frania Tadel, often accompanied Magierowska. I asked Frania about Magierowska and Frania had a high opinion of her. I understood that the two women had made the same proposition to Frania. I asked Frania about it and she was startled that I knew. I explained to her that I had received a similar offer, but that I didn't believe them.

The day of the planned escape from the camp arrived and the two women suddenly demanded that each of us should pay them 5,000 zlotys. We both refused, but pretended that we didn't know one another. The price went down to 2,000 zlotys. Again, we refused.

It seemed that Adamska and Magierowska were prepared to settle for the cash that the Germans were paying for reporting Jews. A cash payment from us was out of the question. The two women apparently wanted to do to us what they had done to Hilda, a fellow inmate from the camp – they had offered her an escape route and then reported her.

It had become cold. With the end of summer, our mood was deteriorating, too. I no longer had the patience to write poems. We no longer sang. The atmosphere had changed. Every day there was an incident. Every day somebody was shot, murdered. Shächter, Haberowa, Hilferding and Löbel – the four Jewish heads of the D.A.W. – had fled, taking the money that people had deposited with them for safekeeping. Shächter left his mother in the D.A.W. barracks, an old woman. Until then the Germans had tolerated her. Now, after Shächter's flight, Gebauer ordered her to smash stones and tasked two orderlies with making sure that she didn't take poison. If she did, they would be hanged. Gebauer then throttled her with his own hands.

The Aryan workshop no longer functioned and the workers were sent to work outside the camp. Frania managed to escape and gave me her address. Two more people from the *Unterkunft* fled and we were afraid of punitive action.

I decided to flee. There was no point to hesitating, because there was nothing to lose.

The next day, at noon, I went to the hospital with a small group of people. A Ukrainian guard opened the door and everyone entered. I was the last in the group, but instead of entering I walked straight ahead!

At the station I climbed into a streetcar. I thought of many possibilities – it was if I were drunk. I nearly succumbed to an extreme weariness, but I tried with all my might not to fall asleep. In Berndyński Square, I went straight to Jadzia Piotrowska's, where Hela Gangel opened the door. Ms. Piotrowska was not yet home so I spoke with Hela in the meantime.

When Jadzia Piotrowska returned, she couldn't believe I had come from the camp. She thought I was still staying with Magierowska and that Mother had gone away. She was surprised that we had not remained in contact.

Unfortunately, Jadzia could no longer help me. Blackmailers had already knocked on her door because of Hela, and she had been forced to ask her to return to her parents. However, Jadzia tried to find a solution to this and went to look for a place for me to stay, but returned empty handed. Meanwhile, I had succumbed to fatigue and had fallen asleep sitting on a chair.

I had to go, so I left Jadzia's house still half asleep. She said that if I wasn't able to stay with Auntie, perhaps she would try again on my behalf. I went to Liczakowski Street, not caring how Auntie would respond to me arriving. I was ready to give my life for the possibility to sleep two days and two nights.

I arrived at number 74, but when I knocked on the front door nothing could be heard from within. I knocked again and turned the door handle. The door wasn't locked. I found Lala in bed in her room, and voices could be heard from the kitchen. I asked Lala if there was anybody at home besides Auntie and Irka, and asked her to call her mother. Lala returned a moment later, not with her mother, but with Nowicka. She pointed to the door and barked, "Get out at once!"

I had expected to get a cool reception, but not something like this. With difficulty, I dragged myself to the streetcar. I stood close to the exit and then I saw Heinen, an SS man and one of the sadists of the camp, with another German. They were not on the road when I descended from the streetcar. I wanted to enter the hospital, but then Heinen appeared on the pavement by the gate. I ran away and entered through the gate of the D.A.W.

Shichman, a Jewish orderly, asked me where I had come from, but then he laughed and said, "Did you escape? It doesn't matter, go to work immediately." The gong sounded and I went straight to the gathering point of the group.

In the camp the *Unterkunft* had been dissolved because of the two who had fled. The following night all the staff of the *Unterkunft* were transferred to the barracks. Another two, who were caught while fleeing, were hanged behind the washroom. Ulrich Jakubowicz, as well as a mechanic and a driver, were locked up in the "cooler".

This was a very sad day in the camp. In addition, the approaching Jewish festivals and the Jewish New Year contributed to the general despondency. I myself was so depressed that the general alarm and panic did not affect me. I understood why everyone was succumbing to death with indifference. I didn't want to live, I was fed up with life. Women were walking around agitated and crying. Olga, the orderly, was crying too. Ala went to the barracks.

I lay down immediately on my bunk and was happy that my wish to sleep in comfort had come true, at least partially. I was exhausted after my failed attempt to escape.

After some time, Bebi – who had come for an inspection – woke me up. "Janka, are you sleeping alone?"

"Only tonight."

When Bebi went away, another woman immediately climbed onto my bunk. I asked her why, upon which she replied that Bebi had sent her here.

"But why? Until now you have been sleeping in barracks 5."

She answered, "That's none of your business. I'm going to sleep here and that's it!"

She threw her bundle of belongings onto the bunk and started to undress. Suddenly, something fell onto my hand from her hair which had been cut short like a man's. I looked at her in disgust. She smiled at me and said it was a wonder that my head was clean – after all this was a camp.

I replied, "You haven't examined my head, but if instead of sucking sweets, you should have bought Cuprex, a preparation against lice like me, so you too would be without lice." I gathered my things and those of Ala, put them onto Olga's bunk, and left the hut.

Outside it was cold and dark, but I didn't feel it. I forgot about the Aryan quarter and about the execution. I was very angry with Bebi, but there was nothing I could do. This woman shared a bunk with the fiancée of the camp policeman, who didn't want to share a bunk with her, so Bebi had organised a transfer. I had been half asleep and had not fought for my place, so it was only my fault. But I wouldn't sleep with her. The light in the hut had already been turned off. I began to shiver, so I returned inside and lay down on the bunk of Lucy, who hadn't returned from the kitchen yet.

The women were making noise and Olga, the *Ordner*, shouted at them and cried. Today she was particularly irritable, being forced to also fill in for Lilka, an orderly who was ill.

Lucy came back when everything had quieted down and most of the women were sleeping. Olga got up and approached us, and Lucy told us the news in a whisper. From tomorrow everybody in the *Unterkunft* would be transferred to the huts, including Orland and his wife, and Ryszard, an *Aksner*. There would be no more showers. Lilka's camp policeman had planned to escape together with her. According to Lucy, Lilka had managed to bribe one of the *Askars,* so he had not intervened when they dug a tunnel under his watchtower. But, the policeman had escaped alone.

When she had finished talking, Lucy whispered to me, "If you have acquaintances, I advise you to escape tomorrow." I began to laugh, remembering my escapades earlier today on the Aryan side. Lucy was astonished by my laughter.

Without saying a word, I showed her my book of tram tickets in which eight were still unused – a memento of my adventures.

Lucy burst out crying and I wanted to comfort her, but how? I understood exactly how she felt. She was now at the difficult stage that I had already passed: the struggle within myself, with my inner voice telling me to live. After returning from Auntie, this voice had become silent.

I was reconciled to my fate, and had become a living corpse, so only I had the courage to go out to the Aryan side while Lucy was afraid to do so. I understood her. She had once been outside of Lvov in the guise of the fiancée of a farm owner, but a friend had reported her. She had spent four months in the Łącki Street prison, and Risiek the *Akser* had saved her from Piaski. She had nowhere to go, so if she went out, she could expect certain death. Therefore it was better that she stayed in the camp, with Ryszek, with Olga, with everybody. I stroked her black, curly hair and tried to comfort her, but I didn't know what to say. I myself was in need of comforting.

11 ROSH HASHANA AND YOM KIPPUR IN THE CAMP - FLIGHT

The next day, Tuesday, was a sad day. On the morning of Rosh Hashana, the sick people were taken out of the hospital – even those who had only come to treat a sore were sent to their deaths.

At noon, I went to the camp to eat. Orland, who had studied to be a Rabbi before the war, greeted us personally and on behalf of the Jewish camp guards he said, "I wish that this year you'll all be free." Everyone cried, Orland himself included. We shook each other's hands.

I approached Orland and said, "May you have satisfaction from your son". This is a traditional Jewish blessing. I wanted to cry, but I was choking and had no more tears. The idea of being free seemed so distant and unattainable. I couldn't imagine myself free.

We returned to the workshop, but there was no work for us. Only the Inspector (*Aufseher*) was present. I was unable to remain seated without working, so I ran away from the workshop. I encountered that Swiss woman, Ms. Magierowska, who stood with her nose in the air – after the dissolution of the "Aryan" workshop, she had remained in the D.A.W. as a supervisor. She greeted me with the words, "Oh, you fool, you could have spent the holidays in Warsaw, but here – just wait for death." "And if instead of traveling to Warsaw, I had ended up in Piaski?" I asked. Then I ran off without waiting for a reply.

I moved around between the huts and wished everyone I met "to be finished with it all soon" or "freedom". I finally became fed up with repeating the same words and just extended my hand in silence. Almost everyone I saw had tears in their eyes.

The holiday brought back memories of how they used to celebrate in the family circle. I, myself, didn't have many memories of the holidays. In our family, before the war, Father didn't pray. Candles were lit only by Grandpa and Grandma. On Yom Kippur, Mother fasted and did not eat together with Father and me.

A year ago, on the day of the Rosh Hashana holiday, I returned to Lvov from Czarny Potok, a village near Lvov. How glad I was to be with Mamoushia again!

I returned to the workshop when the whistle blew, marking the end of the workday. We marched in fives from the workshop to the parade ground. The laundry workers had finished early, and I entered their barrack.

Jakuboviczowa, the mother of Bronek Jakubovicz, who was in charge of the camp laundry, was sitting at the table. Candles had been lit and around her crying women were gathered, wishing her that her son would be set free. She answered them calmly, as if her son was not sitting in the "cooler". I couldn't bear to see this, so I left. In other huts women were crying on their bunks as well.

The weeping went on for two days, then those who had escaped returned. The *Unterkunft* was opened again and the orchestra played during the parade. Jakubowicz was released from solitary confinement and the showers reopened. Those who had escaped received 100 lashes, then were sent to do hard or dirty work.

On the last day before the fast, a party was held in the *Unterkunft* to mark the holidays. On Friday morning, while the German supervisor was absent, we had a concert in the corner – at the table of the "finishing" workers. Elza Kantorska sang, Danka Buchholtz whistled, and I danced with the others. Then I fell asleep under the table. The women were glad that there would be good soup. They knew this because some of the women from the D.A.W. had been sent to work in the kitchen. Orland made sure that we had a festive meal. We had a thick soup of grits with beans and at the entrance to the dining hall, Bebi gave everyone two slices of bread and an apple.

I waited happily for night to fall, so that I could go to sleep without washing immediately after returning to the camp, and sleep another hour because the clocks would be set to winter time.

The next day was Saturday; wash, and then a half day off! When we got back it was already night. The women lit candles and cried while praying. I looked at the flame and began to believe that the Lord could see us. He sees that in spite of the difficult conditions, we praise him and thank him. He wouldn't allow the small surviving group to be killed at the last moment.

I lay down on my bunk. Ala asked me whether I intended to fast. I didn't know how to answer. Fasting is a religious commandment, in memory of the suffering of the Jews, and I was a Jewess like them. I didn't want to probe deeper, because I felt that I would again stop believing in God, because belief expresses hope. I decided to fast.

I woke up and went to the parade ground, where the orchestra played as usual. The D.A.W. columns arranged themselves to go to the showers. For two hours we froze on the parade ground, while they counted us ten times.

Eventually, we got going under the close surveillance of the *Askars* and the camp police; an *Askar* marched in front, together with a Jewish policeman, Borgen, and then came the women orderlies.

We marched swiftly while singing. Some passers-by stared at us, and some followed the good-looking Lilka as far as the bathhouse with their eyes. Borgen, of course, whipped some of the women. Someone, unexpectedly, hit him in the face with his fist. It was Kraut of the D.A.W., a Jew who had been taken to the camp not as an ordinary prisoner, but as an officer – a prisoner of war. We were surrounded by women and Ukrainian merchants, but because of the holiday – Yom Kippur – not one of us bought anything and this time there was exemplary order.

We reached the bathhouse in town and the women stormed the doors, pushing each other, quarrelling about who would get in first. The first column entered. I didn't want to stand and wait, I was already cold and my feet were hurting.

I asked a hairdresser I knew from the dining hall of the *Unterkunft*, who was now an orderly, to let me enter through the front entrance. What a pleasure it was to stand under the stream of warm water. I washed myself. When one group of women had finished, the next group undressed. I relished the warmth of the running water, and didn't want to leave and wait with the other women in the stifling entrance room. I huddled in the corner until the second group had finished and again got under the shower.

Women were quarrelling and pushing each other, ten under a single shower. An *Askar* or a German entered and hit the women, right and left, in order to impose silence.

After we had washed they counted us again. "Miss Frania", as we called Borgen, was not stingy with blows and I, too, was lashed with the end of the whip. But I pretended that nothing had happened; what hurt me more was that I had been beaten by a Jew.

On the way back, there was no longer any order. The *Askars* fired shots to intimidate us and the whip of Miss Frania was used without end. One of the *Askars* even defended one of the women and quarrelled with Borgen.

Back at the camp we immediately went to the dining hall. At the entrance there were the usual pots of soup, but nobody went up to take a portion. Orland gathered us in the dining hall, then ten men entered and prayed together with him. Some women took out sheets of paper with prayers for the dead written on them. There were women who wept.

Instead of praying or weeping, I started to have doubts again about the existence of God. Why should I fast? Were we not deceiving ourselves? Once more I stopped believing.

I returned to the women's camp, but I had no urge to eat and fell asleep. At four in the morning I woke up and ate a slice of bread with sausage with Ala. I was the only one in the barrack who stopped fasting. Ala and Olga never started. Having eaten my fill, I turned onto my side and fell asleep again.

The weather was cold. The orchestra was playing again and the

Unterkunft was functioning. Because of the cold I couldn't sleep at night. Bumek Wahrman and Helena Grün, a poet who wrote in Yiddish, comforted me. They said I was about to go to the Aryan side of the town and then travel to Cracow. I didn't believe them, so my feelings did not change. I couldn't imagine that somebody would make an effort to keep me alive. After all, people only think of themselves. Who cares about a girl called Janina Hescheles and would risk their life for her sake? Without receiving anything in return?

I was in a sorry state. I had lost the will to live. Mother's last words were still echoing in my ears, "Bear your suffering for my sake." These words were the only thing that gave me strength, but I often ignored them with a feeling of resentment towards Mother.

I got the shivers and didn't feel well. I asked a doctor I knew, Dr. Herzl, to add me to the sick-list for a single day and I remained in the hut the whole day. In the evening I went to the *Waschraum* when the workers of the D.A.W. were coming back. Suddenly Rena, who would later be known as Elżbieta, ran towards me, dragged me to one side and whispered, "Boruchovicz [Borwicz] is taking us to Cracow, we go tomorrow!" I heard her, but didn't register what she was saying.

The men arrived back from work. We approached Wahrman and Rena's cousin. Wahrman said to me that tomorrow at 4 o'clock the two of us had to be at the corner of Słoneczna and Szpitalna Streets, near the pharmacy, holding a newspaper. We were to approach a woman with a coloured jacket and to tell her the codeword "Bronek".

The next day, Tuesday, I went to see the Jakubowicz family to say goodbye. Bumek Wahrman, who was also there, told me to be brave. I joined the women from the kitchen of the barracks who were on the way to the bathhouse.

I was not afraid when we left the D.A.W. compound. I moved with difficulty and was sleepy; it seemed to me that I was seeing everything as in a dream. I marched at Rena's side and we went along Szpitalna Street. Zośka Mechanik sang *Ich fuhr a heim* ("I'm going home"). It seemed to me that the lyrics I was hearing were "I'm going back home, back to life".

Behind us marched Eisenberg, Dubs, and the *Werkordner*. The column turned into Rappaport Street, but we kept on straight into Janowska Street. At the meeting point, we encountered Ziutka Rysińska, a Żegota liaison agent, and walked to Wierzbicki. There we also found Bumek, who was cleaning his jacket with milk. Bumek gave us the address of Ms. Winiarska. We slept at her place that night.

From now on I was called Marysia and Rena was called Elżbieta. We kissed each other happily while lying in bed.

On Wednesday we parted from Ms. Winiarska. Ziutka picked us up and told us that Bronek had already gone.

The escape of Rena, her cousin Hala, and myself had not led to any repercussions in the camp, thanks to the underground activists who forged the registry of the camp's inmates. After Bumek had fled, they put his friend from the group of five into solitary confinement, but he was ransomed out.

Elżbieta ordered me around: "Marysia, start walking! Marysia, hurry up! Marysia, sit down! Marysia, get up!" I obeyed her, automatically, like a three-year-old who does what his nanny tells him to do.

When I was sitting on the train, I still couldn't believe that I was traveling to a new life – to Cracow. It seemed to me that I was hearing the bustle of the women in the barracks, the shouts of the orderly Olga Grünfeld, and of Bebi trying to impose silence.

In Cracow I saw Maks Borwicz. In the camp, Mr. S. had asked me to send him his regards, but I forgot. Afterwards we sent a telegram to Bronek. I parted from Elżbieta. She kissed me and automatically I extended my hand.

Ziutka brought me to Mr. Mietek (Mieczyslaw). Mieczyslaw Piotrowski (Peleg) had false papers identifying him as a *Volksdeutsche, an* ethnic German). As a Żegota activist, he was responsible for liaison with the concentration camps.

It seemed to me that I was waking up from a deathly sleep and didn't know where I was. I couldn't imagine that I was in a room, lying in a bed, without anybody breaking the silence.

EPILOGUE

My Lvov is not just my personal story. It is the story of the daily life of the Jewish community in the ghetto of Lvov and in the Janowski concentration camp, from the day the Germans entered the city on 30th June 1941 until a few weeks before the final extermination of the remaining Jews of Lvov and all Galicia in October and November 1943. This makes it a historic document. We should say a few words about the people who played an important role in the life of this community:

In my diary, I mention Dr. Jozef Parnas, the first head of the *Judenrat*, who was 70 years old at the time. He was in charge for barely four months and, after refusing to deliver 500 young men to the Janowski camp as requested, he was arrested, tortured, and shot. His successor, Dr. Adolph Rotfeld, who also failed to fulfil the demands of the Germans, was in bad health and died of natural causes after holding the position for four months. Henryk Landesberg was the third head of the *Judenrat* and, although he obeyed the orders of the Germans, he was hanged from the balcony of the *Judenrat* together with eleven Jewish policemen.

Dr. Maksymilian Kurzrok, who was the head of the hospital in the ghetto and in the Janowski camp, is mentioned several times in the diary. Since his position enabled him to move freely between the two locations, he brought medicines from the ghetto into the camp.

When the ghetto was about to be liquidated, he decided to escape and attempted to save the lives of a number of young hospital employees in the process. Armed with forged documents, the hospital employees were supposed to join the Polish and Ukrainian brigades who were working on the defence fortifications at Dnepropetrovsk. His project failed. Pechesz and Szwadron – two Jews who worked for the Gestapo – recognised Kurzrok at the train station in Lvov and reported the group[1]. They were all shot.

Previously, concerned about the fates of older members of staff who had families, Kurzrok had set up a hiding place in the hospital cellar. This could be reached through the chimney of a stove in the home of Mr. Labiner, in the hope of being able to shelter them during the liquidation of the ghetto. They survived the liquidation, but, having run out of any means of survival, they surrendered to the Germans. They were first brought to the *Frauenlager* but refused to obey an order to get undressed before their execution and collectively swallowed poison. My mother was one of them.

I also mention Ryszard Akser, Bronek Jakubowicz and Abraham Wahrman. Bronislaw Jakubowicz, a prisoner who worked in the *Unterkunft*, was active in an illegal aid organisation in the camp. Akser and Jakubowicz did office work in the *Unterkunft* of the

Janowski camp and – with the help of some of the *Ordner* who were in charge of maintaining order in the camp – they ran a secret aid group which benefitted many prisoners.

Upon arrival, for instance, each prisoner needed to register at the *Unterkunft*. When I was asked about my date of birth, I replied that it was 1931, but Akser wrote down 1929 instead. He added years to the younger ones and made the older ones younger, thereby saving them from instant death. Akser refused all offers to escape. Instead, he stayed in the camp to help his fellow prisoners. He was killed when the camp was liquidated on 19 November 1943.

Abraham (Bumek) Wahrman was a member of Hashomer Hatzair, a left-wing Zionist youth movement. He had been a member of a resistance network, first in the ghetto and then in the camp. He'd managed to obtain some revolvers from Italian soldiers and eventually escaped from the camp but was arrested and killed on the Aryan side.

As to my family: my father was chief editor of *Chwila* (*The Moment*), a daily Jewish newspaper that was published in Polish before the war. *Chwila* was a very popular daily paper with two editions, morning and evening. It was founded in 1919 by Gerszon Zipper, my father's brother-in-law (his sister's husband) shortly after the 1918 pogrom.

The paper also had a literary supplement that was very popular among non-Jews as well as a supplement for children, *Chwilka* (*The Little Moment*). My mother, a nurse by profession, also taught Hebrew. Her family spoke Yiddish and observed religious traditions.

In September 1939, my father and his brother, Mundek, who was also a journalist at *Chwila*, fled Lvov in the face of the advancing Germans. They were convinced that no harm would come to women and children. The two brothers managed to reach Romania and were in Bucharest when they found out that it wasn't the Germans who had invaded Lvov but the Soviets. My father made his way back. He was arrested by the Soviets at the border and spent several months in the Brygidki prison, on Kazimierzowska Street in Lvov, after which he was sent to Russia.

This was a very difficult time for my mother. She would bring parcels to the prison and would often return, exhausted, with a parcel still in her hand. Three months before the German invasion of the Soviet Union (Operation *Barbarossa*), my father returned home. The first pages of the diary describe his return and the short period that we spent together.

When the Germans invaded Lvov, the Soviets retreated and set fire to all the prisons in the city and all the inmates – Ukrainians, Poles, and Jews, criminals and political prisoners – died. The majority of the inmates were Ukrainian.

Many Jews had supported the Soviets during the occupation of Lvov, seeing them as a bulwark against the Germans. So, it was not difficult to blame the Jews for burning down the prisons and to incite the Ukrainian population (with German support) to organise a pogrom against them. It was during this pogrom that my father died, in the same prison in which he had been detained during the Soviet rule.

My Uncle Mundek (my father's brother, who, like my mother's brother, was called Mundek), didn't return home from Romania. Marysia, the woman with whom he had lived before the war, a non-Jew, and their two daughters had remained in Lvov. His daughters were half-Jews, or *Mischlinge* according to Nazi terminology, and therefore of "first degree" Jewish stock. This meant that they were at risk of death. My aunt Marysia had been subjected to blackmail; my presence in her house endangered the lives of her daughters. To protect them, she would say that Mundek was not their father.

It is clear why Aunt Marysia banished me from her house several times. I was too young to understand her behaviour then, and the manner in which I described her in my memoirs was unfair. Eighteen years later, when I became a mother myself, I realised that, in order to protect my children, I may well have done the same.

The pogroms, the spontaneous massacres of Jews by the Ukrainians, were followed by a period of *Aktions*, which were planned massacres of Jews by the Germans. My memoirs are a chronicle of these events, during which my family was decimated.

As often happens, chance determines the destiny of an individual or a group. My mother had attempted, several times, to place me in safety on the Aryan side – outside the ghetto. Each time, it ended in blackmail and I would be returned.

And yet, it was in the Janowski camp where there was no hope whatsoever of making it out, that, as a result of reciting my poems in the women's quarters, I met Michal Borwicz, a prisoner who was a writer and a poet[2]. The *Ordners* of our barracks had alerted him to me. I owe my life to him as well as to many brave Poles. In the Janowski camp, Borwicz was attempting to develop cultural activities that were aimed at instilling a sense of dignity into prisoners in the face of genocide.

Borwicz came from Cracow. When the war broke out in 1939, he was in Lvov on a summer vacation and wound up being cut off from his friends in Cracow, which was occupied by the Germans at the time. His Polish friends were members of the Polish Socialist Party and had prepared for underground activity during the very first days of the war. Some members of this group were Jews operating under false identities and had ties to Żegota, which had been founded by Polish underground organisations.

In 1941, after the German occupation of Lvov, Borwicz's friends managed to find him in the Janowski camp and organised his escape[3]. At that point, Borwicz insisted that they should save other people, too. I was lucky enough to be one of them.

After the escape from the camp, we stayed for a few days with a family in Lvov. We changed clothes, had food and were given false Aryan identities. Then, Ziuta Rysinska, an 18-year-old liaison agent, accompanied us to Cracow.

We spent the first few nights at Maria Hochberg-Mariańska's apartment. She was in charge of finding shelter for us – one of the hardest tasks. I was placed with Wanda Janowska (a beautician), who later married Wladyslaw Wojcik – she was also a Zegota activist. By day, she would receive clients in her apartment which, by night, was used to produce counterfeit Aryan identity papers.

Three weeks after my escape, Mariańska brought me some notebooks and a pencil and asked me to write down my memories. The manuscript was hidden and closely guarded throughout the war. It was then placed in Borwicz's private archives. He in turn transferred them to the archives of the Ghetto Fighters' House in Israel in 1981.

My place of refuge was changed several times. My last address was Jadwiga Strzalecka's[4] orphanage, which had been moved to

Poronin in the Polish Tatras in 1944, after the failed Warsaw Ghetto uprising.

About twenty Jewish children were staying there as well as some Jewish women who had been able to take refuge there as staff. At the end of the war, the orphanage moved to Sopot on the Baltic coast. I stayed there until I graduated from high school. That's when I received a letter from my aunt Mania, my father's sister, who lived in Jerusalem. She wrote that she would be happy to host me, that her home would be my home. The letter sparked yearnings for my family, for those who had perished and those I did not yet know.

The early post-war years in Poland were a time filled with hope. We thought a better world was about to be born. Young people could look forward to their future; we could choose our paths and our studies.

In 1950, after graduating from high school, I left for Israel with a group of legal immigrants. Israel was still a poor country at that time. New immigrants were installed in immigrant camps (*Ma'abarot*). We lived in tents or in huts.

One evening – when I was still living in the immigrant transit camp *Shaar Haaliya* (Immigration Gate) – I made the trip to Jerusalem to visit my aunt Mania. I knocked on her door but no one answered. A neighbour told me my aunt had cancer and was at the Bikour Cholim hospital.

When I went to see her at the hospital that very evening, she recognised me straight away. She took my hand and held it to her lips. "I am so happy to see you," she murmured. I scrutinised her face, looking for similarities with my father's. She had the same grey eyes. It was the first and last time I saw her.

I took a six-month course in Hebrew at an *Ulpan*, a language school located in a kibbutz. The following two years were spent doing compulsory military service. I had given up on the idea of literary studies as my Hebrew wasn't good enough and decided to study Chemistry at the Technicon Israel Institute of Technology in Haifa, while working at the same time to pay for my studies. I lived at Beth Ha-Halutzot (Home for Single Women). There were four or five of us to a room and all our worldly possessions fitted under our beds.

During the last year of my studies, I was able to get a position as a researcher / lecturer. That's when I met Kalman, a young physics lecturer. The Sinai War in 1956, during which Kalman was called up, played a catalysing role in our relationship. Eitan, my first son, was born as I was preparing for my doctorate, and my second son was born when I was finishing it.

Having defended my doctoral thesis, I left for Imperial College in London with my husband and children. At night, when my children were sleeping, I could devote some time to writing a novel, recounting my past. The book, entitled *Hem od Chayim* (They're still alive)[5], published under the pseudonym Tzvia Eitan won a prize in an anonymous literary contest in 1967 organised by the Association of Editors and Composers.

Over the course of my research career, I worked at the Technion Israel Institute of Technology in Haifa, at the Weizmann Institute in Rehovot and at the Ludwig-Maximilian University in Munich. I consider it a great privilege to have been a part of the world of chemistry during the second half of the 20th century.

I ended my professional career at the age of 65, and went on to devote myself to answering the question that had always gnawed at me: how it was possible for the Nazi regime to get to power in Germany of all places – a country that during the 19th and early 20th century could boast a world-renowned scientific community and where the assimilation of Jews was the most extensive in Europe. At the same time, I was fascinated by those who, in Germany, had the courage to resist Nazism. In 2007, after working on it for ten years, my book, *The White Rose – Students and Intellectuals in Germany Before and After Hitler's Rise to Power*[6] was published in Hebrew in Israel.

The 18th-century British historian, Edward Gibbon, wrote: "Human history is nothing but a chronicle of the crimes, follies and misfortunes of man."

Yeshayahou Leibowitz, the Israeli scientist and philosopher, added: "Human history is also a fight against the crimes, against the follies and against the misfortunes of man. That man should emerge victorious from such a battle is unsure, but it is with this battle that the most illustrious pages of human history have been filled."

My diary was first published in Polish in 1946 by the Jewish Historical Council in Cracow[7]. In 1958-1960 it was published in Berlin in an anthology of diaries from the Shoah which appeared in seven editions[8].

The diary went into hibernation for the next 60 years, during which only extracts were published in various languages.

The ice was broken in 2011 when Ada Dianova, director of the Jewish charitable and cultural institute Hesed Arieh, in Lviv in Ukraine, decided to translate and publish the original Polish version of the diary into Ukrainian and Russian, in order to recall the flourishing Jewish cultural life in Lvov before the

Shoah[9]. There followed a spate of publications in other languages[10].

All of these translations had an epilogue in which I recounted the course of my life up to now, after the escape from the Janowski camp.

POEMS BY JANINA 1941-1945

Nostalgia

In a moment of rest,
In a moment of silence
Something persistently whispers in my ears
A moment of past sorrow
Who whispers so? – Nostalgia
When I'm alone,
Someone opens my eyelids
I feel my eyes, filled with tears
What makes them brim over so? – Nostalgia
When my thoughts churn, haltingly
I feel a violent need to cry.
Something takes hold of my heart.
What is it?
Nostalgia.
I long for the happiness past,
When my parents opened up the doors of life

To give me words of love and caresses
What remains of this?
Nostalgia.

The Aryan quarter of Lvov,
September 1942-February 1943.

* * *

The time will come

The days of suffering and pain will end,
Thousands of forsaken corpses
will be piled high behind the barbed wire,
But the day will come,
the time will come
When joy will again reign over us
When, for us too, the sun will shine,
The same sun that now sleeps even in summer.
A song will ring out,
a happy song,
When the clamour of victory will rise up against
The perpetrators of our suffering.
Only then will evil and the pain of existence cease,
Only then will these tormented times come to an end.

The Aryan quarter of Lvov,
September 1942-February 1943.

* * *

So few

So few of our people remain.
Once admired, now trampled on,
These few are tortured in camps,
With no sentence, no right, no hope, only sighs.
These few used to have families,
They knew the happiness of a hearth and home,
Now, that warmth has been stripped away
And we are humiliated.
You preach good deeds and torture the innocent?
If a prisoner dare raise his head
And say even one word, then this madman,
yes madman
(the truth always hurts)
Leads the world with his fists.

Janowski Camp, 1943

* * *

Waisenhof[1]

A small room with a barred window that's called a cell.
Sixty people in it,
share their final hours.
Death nears, lurking in the shadows,
Every minute seems to last a year.
A young boy and girl sit in a corner,
He whispers to her:
I promised you, my love,
That I would never leave you,
And I have kept my promise,
Even death will not part us.

The young girl, crying, replies:
I would have preferred that you be far from me,
I would prefer to be here alone.
The cell door opens,
a woman gets thrown in,
A small child is trailing behind her
He hugs her and whispers:
I'm scared, I don't want to be here,
I want to keep playing,
I'm scared, Mother, I'm scared.
Don't be afraid, my son, don't be afraid,
And she thought to herself:
before they shoot,
I'll cover your eyes with my hands.
The sun goes down.
Exhausted,
People are lying on the floor.
And again the sun rises,
And while the city is still steeped in slumber,
Nine trucks arrive at Waisenhof.
The cell occupants clamber in
And in Piaski their lives come to an end.
One of the prisoners worked in the *Flik*,
Sorting the victims' clothes.
Suddenly, he bent down, shaken,
And clinging to a pink dress,
Picked up a picture of his sweetheart.

Janowski Camp, 1943

* * *

The Piaski sands

What a wonderful view,
the fields, the crimson sun,
The trees on the hill,
And the railway tracks below them.
How beautiful it was here,
during the holidays
When, blissfully free,
we would gather round for a song.
Now, before us, lies the valley of death
A place where our loved ones were torn away from us
And where grey smoke billows above the valley.
The smoke from my mother's bones
and my father's blood
Mixed in with our tears.
Endless sorrow, bitterness and grief.
We, the miserable, contemptible, rejected Jews,
Get dragged around endlessly
To die in the camp.
Before us lie two fields,
The one a field of freedom and life,
The other cloaked in darkness and the shadow of death.
To which are we most drawn?
Can freedom still tempt us
After such extreme suffering,
disappointments and uncertainty?
Who can ease our suffering?
Maybe God can see this from above
How disappointments and failures
go up in smoke in the sands.

* * *

Belzec

What a terrible sight!
A carriage full of people,
In a corner – a few bodies.
They all stand naked,
Their cries drowning out the
The clatter of the wheels –
Only the doomed understand
What the wheels are telling them:
To Belzec! To Belzec! To Belzec!
To die! To die! To die!
To Belzec! To Belzec! To Belzec!
To die! To die! To die!
If you want to live then
Jump! Run! Flee!
But beware!
As the guards stalk you too.
To another doomed person, they whisper:
You'll never see your mother again,
No use in crying,
no use in weeping,
You'll never see your father,
Because the wheels are whisking you away to Belżec –
To Belzec! To Belzec! To Belzec!
To die! To die! To die!
To Belzec! To Belzec! To Belzec!
To die! To die! To die!

The train stops racing,
slowing to a halt.
Cries escape from a thousand hearts
The train has reached its destination.
The whistle blows:
This is Belzec. This is Belzec. This is Belzec.

Janowski Camp, 1943

* * *

To Mother

I feel so bad, it's hard,
Everything weighs on me
But what can I do?
You're so far away.
Sand covers your eyes,
Your beloved heart no longer beats.
Why did you hurt me so?
And leave me on my own,
Surrounded by strangers?
I have to bear my sorrow alone.
But you will surely see me from above,
And keep me from further pain,
And when night falls,
and all around is quiet,
You will come down from heaven,
You will sit on my humble bed,
And as in days gone by,
Kiss my forehead.
I count the hours, the minutes,

Waiting for such a wonderful,
Enchanted reunion.
How happy I will be,
How light and pleasant my soul.
But the moment will be short,
Too short to suffice,
You leave quickly,
This world scares you, I know,
As does the stare of evil people.
Hiding under my covers,
I look for solace.
But such a wonderful night
Makes the pain even worse.
But I think that you'll come back,
That this really happened,
Come, Mother, come,
Come, my beloved.

Janowski Camp, 1943

Night

Night spreads silently, in peace
Quieting and halting the bustle of day
As a mother who appeases and soothes away cares,
Distancing man from the daily grind,
Enveloping the world in darkness,
Cloaking tragedies and suffering with dreams
Until, after slumber is over,
The worries and sorrows return.

Cracow, 16th of July 1944

* * *

Respite

Respite, you are so dear to me as I rest!
Locked away between four walls,
To escape and hide from the city's turmoil
To rest my troubled head in my hands
And escape to other worlds
Towards sweet dreams and infinite visions,
Far, far from men.
This moment of reverie,
Where no one can hear, no one can see,
Is a moment of bliss.
Oh! Comfort me, moment of bliss, comfort me!
Carry me far away
Magic and healing of silence
Moment of bliss, of gentle rocking,
Carry me off to the top of the sky
Where I can live between reality and dream
Where I feel like a little girl again,
Getting away from this miserable earth.

Cracow, 28th of August 1944

* * *

Poronin – on the mountain

Hey! Out of the way!

I've got my skis on
At first, a few jitters,
My legs tremble a bit
I glide down the steep slope
And my skis glide by themselves.
I can feel the power of the wind,
My head is spinning,
Blood pounds through my veins
The wind sweeps through my hair
And pleasantly strokes my cheeks.
Suddenly, one ski twists
And wham!
I'm surrounded by soft whiteness
Covered in snow
I get up quickly
So no one will notice
And take off again, the skis gliding further and further.
After skiing down the steep slope.
And the cloudless blue sky,
Darkened yonder by the forest,
And the Tatra mountain chain
Fills the horizon.
The murmur of the pine trees whispers
Life is worth living
Because the world is wonderful.

The orphanage in Poronin in the Tatra Mountains, January, 1945

ACKNOWLEDGMENTS

Most of the nine translations of my memoirs written in 1946 from the original Polish into other languages were initiated by translators or publishers.

The first full-length translation into German (by Viktor Mika) appeared in seven editions of an anthology of war-time diaries in Berlin in 1958-1960, *Im Feuer vergangen: Tagebucher aus dem Ghetto* (*Perished in the Flames: Diaries from the Ghetto*). An updated edition in German, *Mit den Augen eines zwölfjährigen Mädchens,* was published in 2018 by Metropol, University of Giessen.

The next full-length translations, from Polish into Ukrainian and Russian, were made some 50 years later in 2011, on the initiative of Ada Dianova, director of the Jewish charitable and cultural institution Hesed Arieh in Lviv.

The Jewish population of Lvov was part of the post-war Russian (including Jewish) immigration into Lvov – many apartments were vacant following the extermination of the Jews and expulsion of the Poles. Ada wanted to emphasise the roots of the original Jewish population in the town and organised a full-length theatrical production based on the book, directed by the late Vyacheslav Olkhovskiy. My thanks are due to the Ukrainian historian Yaroslav Hrytsak for his encouragement and support for publication of the diary in Ukrainian and Russian. My appreciation and special thanks are due to Ada for opening up the doors for a renewed interest in my diary. In this, and in all subsequent publications, an Epilogue is included in which I briefly recount my wartime and post-war life in Poland and Israel.

Special thanks are due to Guillem Calaforra (University of Valencia) who translated the diary from Polish into Catalan and Spanish and negotiated its publication in Barcelona and Madrid. I am grateful to him for having drawn attention to Michał Borwicz, whom I cherish, and to whom I owe my life. Guillem also pointed out discrepancies between the 1943 manuscript, preserved in the archives of the Jewish Fighters' House, and the version published in 1946 in Cracow.

My thanks go to Livia Parnes of the Memorial de la Shoah in Paris, for her untiring efforts to have the diary published in French. I thank Catherine Coquio, Professor of Comparative Literature at the Paris-Diderot University, for her invaluable help in having the diary published. I am grateful also to Judith Lyon-Caen, from the EHESS – School of Social Sciences at Paris 6 University for her support for the publication of the diary, and for its inclusion in her seminar programme.

My thanks go also to Agnieszka Żuk for translating the diary from Polish to French, who did not give up even when several publishers refused to publish it. Special thanks are due to Isabelle Vayron for her film *Janina's Notebooks* (*Les Carnet de Janina, Talweg Productions et Vosge Television*), which was used during numerous meetings in France organised by Serge Grossvak to promote the book.

I am grateful to Ewa Kozminska-Frejlak of the Jewish Historical Institute in Warsaw for the many discussions which contributed to the writing of the Epilogue. I also thank Piotr Laskowski for writing an Afterword to the second Polish edition with enlightening comments.

My thanks go to Gideon Gitai for his efforts to have the diary published in Finnish, to Teemu Matinpuro for publishing it and to Tapani Karkkäinen (Helsinki) for his translation from Polish into Finnish.

My translation of the diary from Polish into Hebrew was edited by Michal Kirzner-Appleboim, who polished the Hebrew and showed the corrected manuscript to David Gottesman, head of the Pardes Publishing House. David immediately phoned me and said that he was prepared to publish the diary. My special thanks to Michal for her invaluable support and help, and to David Gottesman for his willingness to publish – which he did within several months.

The cooperative work in preparing the book for publication yielded a solid friendship with Guillem, Michal, Ada, Livia, Ewa and Agnieszka. The theatrical adaptation of the diary (in Polish) in Ukrainian Lviv gave rise to a warm relationship with the actresses Tatyana Sukorkina and Alexandra Somish. My appreciation and thanks go to Bilha Mas-Asherov who prepared a monodrama based on the diary with numerous showings. This, together with the film *Janina*, produced by Chen Shelach for the Ghetto Fighters' House, contributed significantly to the distribution of the Hebrew version of the book. These new friends have enriched my old age.

My thanks go to Anat Bartman-Elhalel, director of the archives of the Ghetto Fighters' House, and to Noam Rachmilevich, for his meticulous maintenance of the manuscript of the diary. I found in them friends who were always ready to help.

My appreciation is due to the Jewish Historical Institute in Warsaw for their initiative to revive their early post-war publications, and thereby to enable their authors to transmit their authentic messages.

The publication of my difficult childhood memories marks the close of my life cycle. My recompense today is happy old age by the side of Kalman, my lifetime companion who, at all stages has stood and stands by my side – for which I can only express my gratitude.

My sons, Eitan and Zwi, have been a constant source of encouragement and support. My special thanks are due to Eitan, Zwi and Serge Grossvak for their contribution to the propagation of my diary in France, to the mayor and council members of Stains, to the municipality of Paris 11, and to the organisations Union des Juifs de France pour la Paix, Ligue des droits de l'Homme, Women in Black and Amnesty International for their contributions.

Dinah McCarthy and Kalman Altman volunteered to undertake a translation into English, based on the Hebrew and French editions, with my occasional intervention when comparison with the original Polish was required. My warm thanks to them for the prodigious efforts they invested in bringing to fruition this English translation.

Finally, I thank my son Eitan for his devoted efforts to find a publisher for this work.

Janina Hescheles Altman

Haifa, May 2019

CITATIONS FROM FOREWORDS, AFTERWORDS AND FILMS

Ada Dianova, Director of the All-Ukrainian Jewish Charitable and Cultural Institute, Hesed Arieh, in Lviv (formerly Lvov).

Excerpt from Isabelle Vayron's film *Janina's Notebooks*, Paris, 2017:

To mark 70 years since the Nazi occupation of Lvov in June 1941 and the first pogrom against the Jews, we considered it necessary to show their important contribution to the cultural and intellectual life of the town before the war.

Therefore, we investigated leading Jewish figures who lived in Lvov before and during the war. We came across the name Henryk Hescheles. He was the editor of Chwila, a newspaper which was published twice a day in Poland. It sold like hotcakes. We discovered that during the war he and most of his family were murdered, but that his daughter Janina had survived. When she arrived in Cracow in 1943, after escaping from the Janowski concentration camp, she began to write down her memoirs in a notebook.

The story was published under the title Through the eyes of a twelve-year-old girl, *Cracow, 1946. The book, written from a child's perspective, is both powerful and terrible. We thought about translating it into Ukrainian and Russian.*

The book tells of so many terrible things. About Ukrainians, too. When I first read this book, I was scared of publishing it. God forbid, I was scared I might trigger a new conflict in Lvov, between Jews and Ukrainians...

* * *

Yaroslav Hrytsak, Professor of History at the I. Franko State University of Lviv.

Excerpt from the Ukrainian and Russian editions, Lvov, 2011:

... Janina Hescheles was lucky to survive. Her memoirs have a rare historic value: they were written while the memories of the Janowski camp were still fresh; they are marked by the photographic precision which characterises the memories of children. One is naturally tempted to draw comparisons with the diary of Anne Frank. But this soon proves to be futile. Anne Frank and her family were in hiding until the German police discovered them in August 1944. Her diary, in fact, teaches us little about the lives of Jews in occupied Amsterdam and the daily life of the Frank family in the concentration camp contrary to the memoirs of Janina Hescheles, where daily life, as well as the violence with which she was confronted from the first days of the war, are the focus. The clandestine life caused Anne Frank anxiety and distress, but her family had access to books, followed a

university course and, with the help of friends, succeeded in obtaining food and distractions. For them, the most frightening things were the explosions they heard from outside.

The life of Janina Hescheles under the occupation presents a violent contrast: besides hearing the echoes of gunfire every day, she witnessed the summary executions of prisoners and, on her way to work, walked along a road strewn with corpses.

Janina was afraid, not of death, but of the fate reserved for children who, instead of being killed on the spot, were buried alive. A passage in her diary reveals a harrowing detail: the prisoners of the camp did not pray for survival, but to be shot so death would be rapid and liberating.

* * *

Guillem Calaforra, University of Valencia, Spain.

Calaforra studied Catalan and Spanish philology at University of Valencia and holds a doctorate in linguistics at the Jagellonian University of Cracow. He is the author of numerous books and behind several translations, including of Janina's diary into Catalan (Barcelona, third edition) and Spanish (Madrid).

Excerpt from the Catalan and Spanish editions:

In 2011, while preparing a Miłosz 100th Anniversary lecture in Cracow and Bucharest, I came across two publications that mentioned the work of a writer unknown to me, Michał Borwicz, an activist in the anti-Nazi underground in Lvov and Cracow.

At the end of the Second World War, Borwicz submitted a doctoral thesis to the Sorbonne, which was published in Paris by the Presses Universitaires de France (1954) and again by

Gallimard (1996) under the name Writings of prisoners condemned to death under the German occupation (1939-1945).

Miłosz praised the book because Borwicz clearly explained the paradox of how the Holocaust distressed victims so much through the industrialised murder of people that they were "shell shocked" and wrote down things and testified in a language that did not transcend clichés and stereotypes.

In his book, Borwicz devoted a chapter to children condemned to death, in which he praises the memoirs of a twelve-year-old girl, Janina Hescheles, who escaped with his help from the concentration camp in Lvov.

Borwicz writes: "Her trustworthy and precise memory, with which she accurately recounts events – we don't know of any similar work which combines so many events with the ability of expression in so few pages. In the manuscript, there are no signs of corrections. On the contrary, the primitiveness of the diary is what gives it its integrity. These notebooks were written when Janina's life was still in danger. Because her attitude to the existing circumstances had not changed, her work is characterised by consistency, corresponding to the realities of her life."

In recent years, many books by witnesses to the Holocaust have been published in Spanish, most of them by adults: Primo Levi, Imre Kertész, Tadeusz Borowski and Elie Wiesel to name a few. The only text of a girl or boy which has been widely published is the diary of Anne Frank, which describes her two-year existence in a secret hiding place in Amsterdam but reveals little of the prevailing anti-Semitic atmosphere at that time. Thus, I decided to look for Janina's book and clarify the question of copyright.

In April 2012, I contacted Yad Vashem in Jerusalem, and received Janina Altman's contact details. I thought this was the daughter of Janina Hescheles, but I got the answer: "No, it is me. It's my diary." This was, for me, the closing of a magic circle.

I was frozen with emotion when I received an email signed Janina Altman. Since then our correspondence has become a source of spiritual nourishment. Janina, a woman who in her youth survived the Shoah, who has been living in Israel since adulthood, is now in her eighties and writes clear and lively letters; and she perseveres in her work for human rights in occupied Palestine. She has given her translator an indelible lesson in humanity, generosity, inner strength and optimism. Thanks to her, her patience and readiness to explain things, the translations into Spanish and Catalan were made possible.

* * *

Ewa Koźmińska-Frejlak, sociologist, regular contributor to the Jewish monthly *Midrasz*, and head of the editorial board of Janina's diary.

Excerpt from the second Polish edition, Warsaw, 2016:

Janina Hescheles was born in 1931 in Lvov, daughter of Amalia and Henryk Hescheles. The text of her diary was written in Cracow in 1943, after the author's escape from the Janowski camp in Lvov. The diary owes its origin, like many other testimonies written during the war on the "Aryan" side, to the initiative of Jewish resistance activists cooperating with Żegota, the Polish Council for Aid to the Jews – in this case, the Cracow branch. The activists encouraged those in hiding to keep diaries and to record their memories from the recent past, providing them with notebooks and pencils. Later, they received additional records and stored and guarded them, moving them from place to place when necessary. They contributed to the emergence of sources documenting the Holocaust, being fully aware of the importance of the material they collected – for future historians, but also for the identity of the Jewish people in general...

In August 1944, the Red Army reached Lublin, the first Polish town to be liberated from German occupation. Jewish historians and writers arrived there and set up a Jewish National Council whose task was to sort through and arrange the documentation of the Shoah. With the Soviet advance, branches of the Council were set up in other towns, too.

In May 1945, the "Hescheles Diary", along with a number of other manuscripts, arrived in Łódź, where the seat of the Central Jewish Historical Commission was located at that time. Later, the diaries were moved to the Cracow branch where the chairman was Michał Borwicz, who had played a part in the escape of Janina Hescheles from the Janowski camp. Borwicz's deputy was Maria Hochberg-Mariańska, in whose care Janina found herself after her escape from the camp, and who, after the war, worked for the Cracow branch of the Commission, and later for Yad Vashem in Israel.

✳ ✳ ✳

Piotr Laskowski, University of Warsaw.

Excerpt from the second Polish edition, Warsaw, 2016:

In addition to the characters that appear in history, heroes and heroines of conspiracy and resistance, there are heroes in these memories that we do not usually talk about: a companion in childish play, a co-prisoner – a companion in camp misery, restless neighbours on the bunks in the hut.

Janina Hescheles records their names carefully and this diary may be the only place where their existence has been recorded, as if this little girl knew and understood that the story as a whole was possible only when every trace, every spark, and every fragment could be preserved. Only in this way can one realise the demanding response of faith that all suffering "somewhere, somehow counts". The words of Janina Hescheles, recorded in the Epilogue to this edition, are not an addition to the memoirs, but an integral part of them: "Today, my Lvov is everywhere."

* * *

Livia Parnes, Historian and cultural activities coordinator at the Mémorial de la Shoah in Paris; co-editor of the French edition of Janina's diary.

Excerpts from the French edition and Isabelle Vayron's film *Janina's Notebooks*, Paris, 2017:

In 2013, at the Mémorial de la Shoah in Paris, an exhibition entitled "At the heart of the genocide. Children in the Shoah 1933-1945" opened. In the beginning of the exhibition, we see yellowed pages from a manuscript in Polish, lent to us by the archives of the Jewish Fighters' House in Israel. We learn that the author was a twelve-year-old girl, Janina Hescheles, who wrote her memoirs a few weeks after escaping from the concentration camp in Janowska Street in Lvov, and that her memoirs (her "diary") were published in Cracow in 1946. That same year, 2013, the archives put the entire manuscript online.

Elsewhere, a philologist in Valencia, Guillem Calaforra, who is working on the translation of the Polish edition of the diary, finds the manuscript in the archives and starts the immense job of comparing it with the published booklet from which, apparently to avoid censorship, all mention of the Soviet occupation of Lvov has been omitted. In Calaforra's translations into Catalan and Spanish, these parts of the diary have been restored, which influences other editions in progress.

The most touching aspect of all these efforts may be the part they probably played in Janina finding the strength, 70 years later, to translate her memoirs into Hebrew and find a publisher.

* * *

Judith Lyon-Caen, Historian, EHESS, School for Advanced Studies in Social Sciences, Paris 6; co-editor of the French edition of Janina's diary.

Excerpts from Isabelle Vayron's film *Janina's Notebooks*, Paris, 2017:

I have been working on Michal Borwicz since 2010. When I read his pioneering book Writings of prisoners condemned to death under the German occupation (1939-1945), published in 1954 in Paris, I became aware of the memoirs of a young girl whom Borwicz calls "Jeannette H." and compares to Anne Frank.

That's how I discovered this testimony. The text is written from a child's perspective. She walks in the street and sees panicked adults coming towards her. This is almost cinematographic: an internal focus on a child who sees panicking adults, people running, shouting... She doesn't immediately analyse the situation from the perspective of adults who tend to instantly contextualise and explain – things occur, this is what is happening.

This text contributes to enabling a public familiar with the Auschwitz model, from France especially, to acquire a different perspective on the experience of organised death. Janowski was a death centre, more than 200,000 people died there, but, located in Lvov's suburbs, it was also a porous space, because some prisoners worked in town and there were several ways out, which actually helped Janina to escape. It was not a death centre sealed off and isolated from everything. On the contrary, so-called "Aryan" Polish women were employed in the D.A.W. workshops where Janina also worked. There is this sort of mix, of porosity... We know of it in an abstract way, but it is very different from the large camp experience of work and death, epitomised for the French by Auschwitz.

Janina's notebooks, if I may say so, enable us to enter the experience of a work camp that is also a death camp, with women's barracks, men's barracks, and an orchestra which plays an important role in what prisoners ironically call "cultural activities"...

So, the reader gets to experience camp life almost at first-hand, although it really can't be called life.

Catherine Coquio, Professor of Comparative Literature, University Diderot, Paris 7, co-author of the book *L'Enfant et le Génocide*, co-director of the series *Literature, History and Politics* by Classiques Garnier, who published Janina's diary.

Excerpts from Isabelle Vayron's film *Janina's Notebooks*, Paris, 2017:

Around 2000-2001, I began investigative research together with Aurélia Kalisky, collecting texts that had been published. We tried to understand the specific resources and behaviours of children during the Shoah. Among these texts, we found Michel

Borwicz's book, Writings of prisoners condemned to death under the German occupation (1939-1945). One chapter focused on the writings of children.

Among the accounts were the notebooks with the testimony of Janina Hescheles and Anne Frank's diary. We were struck by the very great difference between them. Anne Frank's text is not devoid of violence. It has a sense of foreboding and longing for protection, but that of Janina immerses us completely in the worst kind of violence.

So, finding this story, which was written by a child who had survived all this, was absolutely extraordinary. For many reasons, this testimony is exceptional and its author is, too.

Michal Borwicz and Janina were in the same Janowski camp in a suburb of Lvov, near the ghetto. At that time, he was about 30 years old, a writer and a poet. He later became a historian. He heard the little girl, whom he had been told about previously, recite her poems in the camp, near the women's barracks, and it caught his attention. This text has a very rich and moving history because it was collected and saved, just like the girl was saved. It was later published by the very man who had saved it.

The texts of the survivors, especially those of children, move us enormously. Indifference becomes impossible when we read such writings. To me, therefore, they seem extremely precious, maybe even more so than the third and fourth generation literature which, although essential, doesn't have the same power to mobilise and shake us.

I know that Janina is angry, more than angry actually, about the current policies of Israel. Although she may use phrases that might sound exaggerated, it is important that this anger is heard in the book. It is an aspect of her personality. The young Janina would not have written in the way she did if the intensity of how she experiences things was not an integral part of her personality.

* * *

Michal Kirzner-Appleboim, translator, editor, writer; editor of the Hebrew edition of Janina's diary.

Excerpts from the Hebrew edition, Haifa, 2016:

It is seldom that the work of editing books leads to unexpected human contact. When I received an e-mail request from someone called Janina to edit the Hebrew version of the diary she had written during the Shoah, I had no idea that both the text and the person would leave such a deep impression on me.

The door to her house was opened by a small, lean woman, resembling a twelve-year-old girl. But make no mistake, this woman was stronger than the metals on which she had worked in her long years as a research chemist.

Janina's diary, beyond its historical importance as a testimony written in real-time, is a paean to the spirit of man which is stronger than all the forces of darkness. Janina was exposed in her childhood to unimaginable cruelty and lost all her loved ones, but there were two things that the war couldn't take from her: her belief in man and hope.

Her belief in man is a guiding light for Janina, a veteran activist for human rights, for equality and for peace. As to hope – it is almost unbelievable that a woman who in her childhood experienced the most terrible things managed not only to piece together the shattered fragments of her life so admirably, both personally and professionally, but even to state that "life is beautiful". What a lesson this is for all of us.

* * *

Helena Ganor, survivor of the Holocaust in Lvov, retired medical practitioner in southern California, author of the book *Four letters to the witnesses of my childhood.*

Excerpts from her book, Syracuse University Press, 2007:

In the ghetto during the Nazi occupation, one of the older girls, whose name was Janka Hescheles, organised a theatre and we all took turns playing some imaginary roles. Her father had been an editor at an important newspaper in Lvov before the war. All of us were delighted at this imaginary flight from our grim existence.

After the war, she published a book about these times, Through the eyes of a twelve-year-old-girl. *I have this book which I brought with me to America. Father bought it for me after the war, because she wrote about me, naming me by my first and last name and thus making me more than just an anonymous girl who had survived this nightmarish time.*

The book as I see it now was a Polish equivalent of The Diary of Anne Frank. *How sad it is that this book is unknown in the world. It isn't known because this girl unwittingly painted less than a noble picture of the country we once called ours. Thus, the people did not want to "spread the news" and popularise her book.*

NOTES

Introduction

1. Ziuta Ryshińska, Żegota liaison agent. She was eventually captured and sent to the Plaszow concentration camp and from there to Auschwitz. She survived the war and received the Yad Vashem Righteous Among the Nations award.
2. Jadwiga Strzałecka founded an orphanage in Warsaw in which she concealed some ten Jewish children and a number of Jewish women who worked with the children. After the destruction of Warsaw, many people remained without identity papers and the orphanage took in many more Jewish orphans and women workers. No one besides Jadwiga knew the identity of the inmates.
3. Maria Hochberg-Mariańska (Miriam Peleg was the name she adopted in Israel), journalist and Żegota (Council for Aid to Jews) activist. Hochberg-Mariańska subsequently worked with orphaned children, collected testimonies, and performed duties for Yad Vashem in Israel. Her books include among others: *The children accuse,* eds. Maria Hochberg-Mariańska, Noe Grüss (in Polish), Cracow, 1947; and *Outside the ghetto walls in occupied Cracow,* co-authored with M. Ben-Zvi (in Hebrew), Yad Vashem, 1987.
4. Janina Hescheles, *Oczyma dwunastoletniej dziewczyny,* Wojewodzka Żydowska Komisja Historyczna, Cracow, 1946. Editorial committee: Michal Borwicz, Maria Hochberg-Mariańska, Jósef Wulf.

1. Father comes Home

1. *Chwila* was a very popular daily paper with two editions, morning and evening. It was founded in 1919 by Gerszon Zipper, my father's brother-in-law (his sister's husband), shortly after the 1918 pogrom. The paper also had a literary supplement that was popular among non-Jews, as well as a supplement for children, *Chwilka (The Little Moment).*

5. On the Aryan side

1. Piaski – "the sands": Many of the prisoners frm the Janowski camp were shot and burnt in the Piaski sands, adjoining the Janowski camp.

8. Separation from Mother

1. This information was passed on to me by Ms. Adlersberg, a relative of Kurzrok.

9. In the D.A.W. and the Janowski camp

1. Michal Borwicz (Maksimilian Boruchovicz, pseudonym Ilian), initiated the cultural activity in the camp and was in contact with the Polish underground – the Counsel for Aid to the Jews (Zegota).
2. Bronek Jakubowicz worked in the *Unterkunft*, was part of the aid network and in contact with the Polish underground outside the camp.
3. Yerachmiel Grün, a poet who wrote in Yiddish, was later killed in the camp.
4. David Fränkel, a journalist, militant socialist and member of Hashomer Hatzair, was also later killed in the camp.
5. Perec Kleinmann, a painter and stage decorator, was also later killed in the camp. Grün and Kleinmann were celebrities at the Yiddish theatre in Lvov.

10. The Hanging

1. Bumek (Abraham) Wahrman, a member of the Hashomer Hatsair movement and active in underground work in the Lvov ghetto and the Janowski camp, obtained pistols from Italian soldiers. He escaped from the camp but was caught and shot on the Aryan side.

Epilogue

1. This information about the attempt of Kurzrok to save the older members of the hospital staff was passed on to me by his relative Ms. Adlersberg.
2. Michal Borwicz was known as a writer before the war and during the war wrote poetry. His poems can be found in the anthology *Piesn ujdzie calo. Anotlogia wierszy o zydach pod okupacja niemieck* (Central Jewish

Historical Commission, Warsaw, 1947, pp. 60-70). After the war he founded the Jewish Historical Commission in Cracow, which collected testimonies and published books. In 1953 he received a doctorate in Sociology at the Sorbonne in Paris.

3. Thanks mainly to Mieczyslaw Piotrowski (known later in Israel as Mordechaï Peleg), a Żegota liaison agent between Cracow and Lvov.

4. Jadwiga Strzalecka saved dozens of Jewish children as well as Jewish women who worked with the children in the orphanage. When the orphanage was still in Warsaw, it was inspected by German experts who carried out "anthropological tests" to determine if any of the children were Jewish. They didn't find any.

5. Published under the pseudonym Tzvia Eitan (based on the names of my children), by Alef in Tel Aviv, 1969.

6. Janina Altman, *Havered Halavan* (*The White Rose*), Pardes, Haïfa, 2007. The first part of this work was published in German: Janina Altman, *Naturwissenschaftler vor und nach Hitlers Aufstieg zur Macht,* Amazon (Kindle), 2013.

7. Janina Hescheles. *Oczyma dwunastoletniej dziewczyny*, Wojewodzka Żydowska Komisja Historyczna, Cracow, 1946.

8. Janina Hescheles, *Mit den Augen eines zwölfjährigen Mädchens*, in: Im Feuer vergangen, *Tagebücher aus dem Ghetto*, Verlag Rutten & Loening, Berlin, 1958, pp. 299-357.

9. Ukrainian: Яніна Гешелес. *Очима дванадцятирічної дівчинки*. Переклав Андрій Павлишин, Дух і літера, Kiev, 2011; Russian: Янина Хешелес. *Глазами двенадцатилетней девочки*, Перевод Владимира Каденко, Дух і літера, Kiev, 2011.

10. Catalan: Janina Hescheles. *Amb els ulls d'una nena de dotze anys,* Riurau Editors, Jaume Ortolà, Barcelona, 2012 (3 editions).

Spanish: Janina Hescheles. *Con los ojos de una nina de doce anos,* Hermida Editores, Madrid, 2014.

Finnish: *Janinan päiväkirjät*, Like, Helsinki. 2015.

Polish, updated 2nd edition: *Oczyma dwunastoletniej dziewczyny,* Central Jewish Historical Commission, Warsaw, 2015.

Hebrew: Janina Hescheles. בעיני ילדה בת שתים-עשרה, Pardes Publishers, Haifa, 2016.

French: *Les Cahiers de Janina* (Janina's notebooks), Classiques Garnier, Paris, 2017.

German: Janina Hescheles, *Mit den Augen eines zwölfjährigen Mädchens,* Metropol, University of Giessen, 2019.

Poems by Janina 1941-1945

1. A prison for Jews in Waisenhof Street in Lvov, from which most prisoners were taken to their death.

KIND REVIEW REQUEST

Dear Reader,

If you have enjoyed reading *My Lvov*,
please do leave a review
on Amazon or Goodreads.
This would be very much appreciated.
Thank you!

Janina Hescheles

GLOSSARY

Italicized names refer to people mentioned in these memoirs,

Arbeitsamt - the Jewish labour office

Askar – a Ukrainian guard

Aufseher – inspector

Ausweiss – identity card

Belżec – extermination camp

Brygidki – prison in which Henryk Hescheles was killed

Bügler – ironer

Chwila (The Moment) – Jewish daily newspaper in Polish of which Henryk Hescheles is chief editor

D.A.W. (Deutsche Ausrüstungswerke) – German armaments works

Einsatz Kommando – Special Operations Force

Esskarte – food vouchers

Frauenlager – women's camp

Gelände – open space in the D.A.W. in which the men's camp was situated

Haushalt – household certificate

heraus – get out

Judenrat – Jewish Council

Jüdenrein – Free of Jews

Jüdischer Ordnungsdienst – Jewish militia

Julag (Jüdischer Arbeitslager) – Remains of the ghetto, in which workers still lived

Kolonnenführer – head of the column

Kontrolstube – security hut

Lagerpolizist – camp policeman

Lemberg, Lvov, Lviv – Austrian town (Lemberg) before WWI, Polish between WWI and WWII, Ukrainian (Soviet) after WWII

Meldekarte – a registration card from the *Arbeitsamt* or Jewish labour office

Mémorial de la Shoah – Shoah memorial centre in Paris

Mischling – Descendant of mixed Aryan and Jewish parents or grandparents

Ordner, Werkordner – orderly, work orderly

Piaski – "the Sands", place of mass executions and burning of bodies, near Janowski camp

Rohstoff – a recycling company of 'raw materials'

Sanitätspersonel – health worker

Scheisskarte – permit to go to the latrine

Schupo (*Schutzpolizei*) – policeman

Sonderdienst – Special Service

Technion-Israel Institute of Technology (*Haifa*) – where Janina studied Chemistry and obtained her doctorate

Todbrücke – Death Bridge

Unterkunft – A German administration office that ran the *Julag*

Wachmänner – German watchmen

Wannsee Conference – where Nazi leadership adopts resolution for the "Final Solution of the Jewish Question"

Waisenhof – Prison run by Jewish police

Wäscherei – hut of laundry workers

Waschraum – washroom

Wehrmacht – German armed forces

Wohnungsamt – Housing authority

Żegota – Council for Aid to Jews

Zurichter – person who prepared material to be sewn

Zwangsarbeitlager – forced labour camp

INDEX

Italicized names and places are used when they appear in these memoirs.

Brat (husband of Bronia, editor and then clerk)

Calaforra, Guillem

Coquio, Catherine

Dianowa, Ada

Fränkel, David

Ganor, Helena

Gebauer

Gottesman, David

Grossvak, Serge

Grün, Helena and Yerachmiel

Hasenus Lucy

Hescheles (Blumenthal), Amalia (Lusia, Mother, Mamushia)

Hescheles, Henryk (Father, Tatusch)

Hescheles, Janina (Janka, Janula, Yania)

Hescheles, Mundek (Father's brother)

Hirsch, Jacob (Janina's cousin)

Hochberg-Marianska, Maria (Marysia)

Hrytsak, Yaroslav

Jakubowicz, Bronislaw (Bronek)

Janowska (Wójcikowa), Wanda

Jolles, Dr.

Karkkäinen, Tapani

Kirzner Applebaum, Michal

Kleinmann, Perec

Kordybowa

Kozminska-Frejlak, Ewa

Kurzrok, Maksymilian

Labiner

Landesberg, Henryk

Laskowski, Piotr

Levin, Rabbi

Lyon-Caen, Judith

Marianska (Maria-Hochberg)

Matinpuro, Teemu

Marysia, Aunt (mother of Irka and Lala)

Mas-Asherov, Bilha

McCarthy, Dinah

Miłosz, Czesław

Nowicka

Olga

Orland

Parnas, Jozef

Parnes, Livia

Pietrowska, Jadzia

Piotrowski, Mieczyslaw (Mietek)

Rachmilevich, Noam

Rena (Elzbieta) Aiden

Rotfeld, Adolph

Rysińska, Ziuta

Shelach, Chen

Somish, Sasha (Alexandra)

Strzalecka, Jadwiga

Sukorkina, Tatyana

Szeptycki (Archbishop), Andrij

Tadanier, Dr.

Vayron, Isabelle

Wahrman, Bumek/Bronek (Abraham)

Warzok

Zipper, Mania (Miriam)

Żuk, Agnieszka

Printed in Great Britain
by Amazon